PARROTISMS

THE AUTOBIOGRAPHY

OF

Ian Parrott

BRITISH MUSIC SOCIETY
Monograph No.5

2003

This publication is copyright and may not be reproduced in any way, copied into a database or mounted on the internet without the permission of the copyright owner and of the British Music Society.

© Ian Parrott, 2003

The author has asserted his right under the Copyright, Designs and Patents Act, 1988, to be identified as the Author of this Work.

ISBN: 1 870536 24 X

Published by the British Music Society,
7 Tudor Gardens, Upminster, Essex RM14 3DE

British Library Cataloguing in Publication Data

A CIP record for this book is available from the British Library

Acknowledgements

Influences on My Music is printed by permission of *Musical Opinion*

Globetrotting is printed by permission of *The Western Mail*

Thirty-three Years in Welsh Music is printed by permission of the Welsh Music Guild

The Coventry Madonna and Bach is printed by permission of *The Musical Times*

An Introduction to Warlock is printed by permission of the Peter Warlock Society

The quotation from the Wind Quintet No.2 on page 43 is by permission of the publisher, Phylloscopus Publications

The author wishes to record his thanks to Roger Carpenter for his meticulous editorial work in preparing this book for publication

Printed by The Arc & Throstle Press Ltd.,
Nanholme Mill, Shaw Wood Road, Todmorden, Lancs OL14 6DA

Contents

Page

Part One — Growth

I	Ancestors	1
II	Early Days	3
III	School	7
IV	Royal College of Music	10
V	1933	11
VI	Music Scholarship and Germany	13
VII	Oxford	14
VIII	1937	17
IX	Malvern	19

Part Two — Love and War

I	Old Tithe Barn	23
II	Overseas	25
III	Egypt	26

Part Three — The Academic Life

I	Aberystwyth	29
II	The Guild for the Promotion of Welsh Music	30
III	Postlude	32

Page

Appendices

			Page
1	Articles		
	(a) *Influences on My Music*		38
	(b) *Globetrotting*		48
	(c) *Thirty-three Years in Welsh Music*		51
	(d) *The Coventry Madonna and Bach*		63
	(e) *An Introduction to Warlock*		66
2	80th Birthday Concert Programme		68
3	Diary of Events		70
4	Compositions		76
5	Recordings		96
6	Writings, etc		97
Index			101

Illustrations

Horace Bailey Parrott, c1930	4
Muriel Annie Parrott (née Blackford), c1910	6
Ian, aged $3^{1}/_{2}$ months, held by his grandfather	7
The Home Boarders' Group, Harrow School, 1931	8
Oxford University Gazette, December 4th 1940	24
Ian & Elizabeth Parrott, Aberystwyth, 1950s	30
Llanbadarn Church by Elizabeth Parrott	33
Ian & Michael Parrott with Paddy Ashdown, Montacute, July 3rd 1993	34
Ian & Jeanne Parrott, Christmas 1995	37
The opening of the Wind Quintet No.2	43
Ian & Elizabeth Parrott with Yehudi Menuhin, Worcester, c1970	53
Once upon a Time: the Aberystwyth performers, November 1961	54
Ian & Elizabeth Parrott at the British Music Information Centre, March 1986	61
Vice-Presidents of the Elgar Society, Malvern, June 4th 1988	73
The portrait by Daphne Todd, 1991	74
Ian Parrott playing Chopin's Pleyel at Villa Medici Giulini, May 1999	75
Fanfare-Overture: a passage from the autograph score	80-81
Arfon: page one of the autograph	86
The 80th Birthday Concert, Machynlleth, March 5th 1996	92

The cover photograph of Ian Parrott, taken on September 29th 2002, is reproduced by kind permission of Robin Gwyndaf.

The music on page 107 is from the autograph of the final bars of *Portraits*.

Part One — Growth

I Ancestors

Our family name is Norman-French in origin and the spelling varies in many ways from Perrot (Little Peter, also 'Pierrot') to Parat and Parrott. It comes probably from a castle in Brittany, whence William de Perrott in 957 made an expedition to Somerset, where the river is now called the Parrett. This man's grandson was knighted by William the Conqueror. Many of these Perrots settled in South Wales and Sir Andrew Perrot built Narberth castle in about 1246.

My grandfather, Joseph Erichson Parrott (1846-1931), used to say that our family was descended from an illegitimate son of Henry VIII. It can be supposed that this was Sir John Perrott, born at Haroldston, Pembrokeshire in 1527, reputed son of Sir Thomas Perrott but said to be the natural son of Henry VIII and Mary Berkeley, but it seems more likely that our branch comes from the other line of Perrotts, also of Haroldston, represented by Robert Perrott in the sixteenth century, who will be discussed below.

However, some words must first be said about Sir John, who was one of the most colourful members of the family. One of the outstanding personalities of South Wales at the time, he shared with Master Richard Vaughan of Whitland the Queen's commission "for the apprehension of pyrats". No nice distinction was made in those days between catching pirates and performing acts of brigandage oneself. As Roland Williams points out in *Some Studies of Elizabethan Wales* (Newtown 1924), piracy was regarded more as an offence against the individual, and a *"species of piratical pilfering became an almost lawful side-issue of maritime trade. Such acts of piracy were not considered to entail any stigma upon the adventurer even when undertaken against his own countrymen."* And says GDJ in 'Elizabethan Haverfordwest' in *The Pembroke County and West Wales Guardian*, February 12th 1954, *"many a tun of gascon wine found its way to the cellars of Sir John"*. A complicated feud existed for a long time between Perrott and Vaughan, the men of Laugharne, Carmarthenshire, taking sides with Sir John and acting as a continual thorn in the flesh to Vaughan. Frequently the cry was "Sir John Perrott is upon us!", and the pirates — or men unfortunate enough to be on the wrong side — were put in the gaol (of which Sir John was Keeper) at Haverfordwest, where there is a road to this day called Perrott's Road. Also there are the remnants of the fine house belonging to Sir John, who was a great benefactor to the town.

In 1552 he was sharply bidden by the Admiralty to send up to London one Philip ap Rice, a pirate, and in 1565 he was reprimanded for the "marvellous insufficiencye" of his deputy, John Perrott of Tenby (who was he?), who had bungled the arrest of certain pirates. He was imprisoned by Queen Mary for harbouring Protestants but later was granted the Lordship and Castle of Carew, which lies a few miles north of Tenby. The north wall of the castle was rebuilt and extended by Sir John to transform it from a barracks into an Elizabethan mansion. He was made a Knight of the Bath by Edward VI.

From 1570 to 1575, Sir John Perrott was President of Munster, and from 1584 to 1588 he was Lord Deputy of Ireland, where he became noted for his arbitrary ways and fierce temper. On his return from Ireland he was given many favours by Queen Elizabeth. It was thought that, in order to avoid the English Fleet, the Spanish Armada would seek a landing at Milford Haven, and in July 1588 Sir John Perrott was appointed to defend this garrison. However the Spaniards never came to Milford.

As a young man Sir John Perrott was a good athlete and later was known for strength, courage and for his "port and majesty of personage", resembling his reputed father closely in looks, voice and ways. He was a gallant soldier, and Rawlinson, in his history of 'That Eminent Statesman' (1728), describes him as a *"Man in Stature very tall and bigg, exceeding the ordinary Stature of Men by much ... his Eye was marvellous percing"*. He was resolute in danger and faithful to his friends but immoderate in his language. Fenton in *A Historical Tour through Pembrokeshire* (1811) quotes: *"Doctor Swift in the preface to his Polite Conversation says that Sir John Perrott was the first who swore by G—'s w—k—rs"*.

In 1591 falsely accused of high treason by Thomas Cadarn, he was sent to the Tower of London, finally preventing him from maintaining as he would have wished the improvements at Carew Castle. Queen Elizabeth refused to sign the death warrant, as she believed him innocent, and he died a natural death in the Tower in 1592. [Some of the above information is from Percy C C Evans's MA thesis on Sir John in 1940]

A mention now of Robert Perrott is interesting as the evidence shows descent without realisation of the musical connection. He was the first Welshman to get the degree of D.Mus. The son of George Perrott of Haroldston, he died in Oxford in 1550, organist of Magdalen. His sons were Simon, 1532, and Clement. These members of the family were cousins of Sir John Perrott. The Yorkshire Perrots, including George Perrot (1710-1780), Baron of the Exchequer, spring from this line. *The Dictionary of National Biography* suggests that Sir Richard Perrott, who died in 1796, baronet, eldest son of Richard Perrott of Broseley in Shropshire, was descended from this Haroldston branch, though Fenton does not consider the claim well-founded. This Sir Richard Perrott, whose portrait was engraved by V Green in 1770, obtained foreign decorations and was honoured by Frederick the Great in 1753. A letter from a Mr A G Barrett to my uncle, William Alfred Erichson Parrott (1872-1949), states:

> *"I have the names of a number of Parrotts and Perrotts — Doctors, Ministers and Soldiers, but as there were children of both Sir Richard Perrott, Baronet, and of Dr James Parrott — Sir Richard's brother — it is something of a puzzle to decide from which of the two Brothers the present families descend, but I think it is now definitely settled by old letters that those brothers are the ancestors of the families with which you are connected, and possibly myself."*

As will be seen below, it is obvious that what was wanted here was something suggesting a medical history. Certainly there was little interest in music in my grandfather's family, and it is curious that there should be this clear return four hundred years later to music — for I also became a doctor of music of Oxford University.

II Early Days

Benjamin Goddard Perrott married Mary Barnes on July 25th 1780 at Wisborough Green, West Sussex. They had 24 children, and my great-grandfather, Augustus Alfred, born 1805, was the youngest of these. One of Augustus's elder brothers was a colonel in the Carabineers in the Sudan, another being tutor to the Duke of Orléans. Mr John Franklin of Sydney, Australia, pieced together in 1991 a chart with most of these names, he being descended from the eldest, William Perrott, born 1782. Augustus Alfred became a druggist in Twickenham and married Frances

Neighbour in Paddington on October 25th 1840. After his death in Twickenham in 1849, his widow married into the Webb family. His children included my grandfather, Joseph, and Alice, whose grandchildren, Alice, Margaret and Jane Clarke, have been friends as well as contemporaries. A rich man promised to leave Joseph Parrott all his money if he took his name of Erichson. This was done, but the money did not appear!

Joseph, teaching at Stockwell in South London, wrote in his diary on January 26th 1863, at the age of seventeen: *"... back to School to hear a lecture on English Music delivered by Mr Coward one of our first English composers which was illustrated by some first class professionals it was well worth hearing and as good as a 'Hampton Court' concert"*. He was offered organ lessons for fifteen shillings per year and practised a certain amount, but his main inclinations were towards chemistry, which he studied assiduously every evening, and sketching. This led to his becoming a medical doctor, in Dulwich and Epsom, with oil painting as one of his hobbies. Other entries in the diary included seeing a balloon ascent at the Crystal Palace, *"containing some gentlemen and a lady"*, and making *"oxygen for lime light"*. References to Mr Bailey and Horace suggest a friendship which was commemorated when he later named his youngest son Horace Bailey Parrott.

Horace Bailey Parrott, Ian's father, c1930

Each son developed in a different way; William Alfred Erichson (1872-1949), who liked the idea of a medical career even less than most and, Berlioz-like, paced the streets instead of attending the hospital, went to Australia and became a clergyman; Charles Montague (1875-1952) became a painter, studying in Paris, and also went to Australia; Hugh MacDowall (1876-1943), who took his second name from his mother's side of the family, where there was Indian blood [1] mixed with the Scottish, actually took up the favoured profession of medicine; Joseph Reginald (Rex), born in 1878, went into an insurance company; Dorothy Mary (1881-1941) married Phillip Henry Pring; and Horace Bailey, my father (November 27th 1883 - August 4th 1953), after many experiences in various branches of marine and civil engineering, joined the British Oxygen Company. Eventually, in 1918, this meant that we moved from Streatham to the north side of London and settled in Harrow.

Thus my father and great-grandfather were the youngest of large families. It has been the custom of the western world to heap honours on the first-born, but certain not-so-primitive tribes believe, with a good deal of sense, I should say, that the maturest qualities of the parents go into the last-born. Certainly my father was wonderfully endowed with kindness, patience, thoughtfulness and wisdom. Although my father had a good singing voice, my uncle Hugh had a really fine operatic baritone, which was regrettably confined to private round-the-piano recitals.

My mother, whose maiden name was Muriel Annie Blackford, born September 9th 1883, traces her descent from Andrew Andrew, a Master Weaver of Exminster, Devon, whose ancestors were knighted on the field of Agincourt. Her father, John Richard Blackford of Calne, Wiltshire, born in 1845, was a mathematician and, like my paternal grandfather, was also a painter, but he preferred watercolours. His wife, descended from the Andrew family, Mary Amelia Louisa Tuck, born 1844, won a harmony prize at an early age and passed on a love of music to my mother. Trained by Miss Lucy Hillier, my mother gave a particularly successful piano recital in Sutton in April 1907.

My father and mother were married at Streatham Hill in 1913 and during the First World War, with snow on the ground, I was born there on 5th March 1916, but my earliest recollections are of 14 Kenton Road, Harrow, where I spent the early impressionable years. One of these was meeting a bull which I described as a "cow with wewy fat cheeks". My inclination was strongly towards the visual, and several books were filled with drawings. These showed, I think, a fair degree of imagination as well as invention, and every new subject studied at school had to be drawn into the fantasy; a new world was designed with a map, a new language with tables of declensions in the manner of the Latin grammar and an invented history. At Miss Orton Smith's 'dame' school I was naughty, frightened the little girls, pushed a boy into a pond and broke some brand-new coloured pencils. No doubt my father was relieved when I was put under the severer discipline of Orley Farm Preparatory School (now the Purcell School) in 1924. Soon after this the family moved a short distance to South House, Flambard Road; my sister, Cynthia, having been born two years earlier.

Muriel Annie Parrott (née Blackford), Ian's mother, c1910

I had already at the age of seven been so enthralled by my mother's playing of the music of Beethoven, Chopin and Liszt, that I started composing piano music on my own account. My mother felt that I was troubling too much over such mysteries as demisemiquavers, but was unable to quench my zeal, and by the age of ten I was writing sonatas.

The visual urge had its last serious chance at this time when, in September 1926, we visited Caudebec-en-Caux in Normandy, and I produced a number of sketches and paintings. Although sketching was to be a hobby for many years, there seemed no doubt about the genuineness of my musical bent, so my parents encouraged it in every way possible, including the starting of violin lessons which was invaluable for the ear. Before entering Harrow School at the end of 1929, I had a course of harmony lessons with Benjamin Dale, which further helped in the right direction.

Ian, aged 3½ months, held by his maternal grandfather, John Richard Blackford

III School

From the autumn of 1929 to the summer of 1932 I was a day-boy at Harrow and cannot say, looking back on it, that I was on the whole happy. All schools, and public schools no less than most, seek to mould boys to a pattern, and any individual talent in music would receive lukewarm encouragement. Once I showed an unfinished composition to the Director of Music, Dr Thatcher (later Sir Reginald, died 1957), and he said: "I do not want to pour cold water, but I wouldn't bother to finish that piece if I were you". This aloof treatment did, however, harden my determination to get on by my own efforts, and at least Thatcher's taste in music was so wide as to open many paths and develop any of the broadmindedness which I now may possess. A more vivid memory than the school music-making was the first trip in 1931 to my mother's old teacher at Calne, Mr William Pullein. He said that a pianist's technique could be founded on two composers: Chopin and Bach. It was the latter who was new to me, and, as I was studying the organ as well, a great new world of music was opened, the foundations of a tremendous enthusiasm for Bach being laid. I was also able to admire the magnificent 5-manual organ in the Parish Church and the no less resplendent replica in the private house of the donor, a member of the Harris family of the famous Harris's bacon.

The Home Boarders' Group, Harrow School, 1931 [Ian back row far right]

Other enthusiasms were established in this year. Gilbert and Sullivan to me means ninety per cent Sullivan, and in 1931 I saw both *The Mikado* and *Iolanthe* as well as a laboured imitation of the manner: *Tantivy Towers* (Dunhill). Again in the year in which I shaved for the first time I heard Tchaikovsky's Sixth Symphony and immediately arranged the 5/4 movement for the chamber ensemble which was available at the time. The standby of our music-making was Norman Strachan with his violin. Despite the fact that I had knocked him down in the snow on our first meeting, we became firm friends. His elder brother played the clarinet, and John Iago played the flute. Other instruments came and went, and occasionally my father was called in to deal with the dinner gong in E flat. The scoring of the domestic concertos which I wrote thus varied. At school I was learning flute, organ, harmony and piano and played in a quintet of violins an *Allegro* by Fiocco in the December concert. I also heard and enjoyed Holst conducting *The Planets*. After swotting *Brahms* by Specht and *Franck* by d'Indy, I managed to win the Briscoe Eyre second prize. Early the following year I wrote a long account of hearing Isolde Menges play Bach's Violin Concerto in A minor, saying that it completely overshadowed Brahms's Third Symphony which came before. Perhaps my aversion to Brahms started here, just as people dislike the Scott novels which they were forced to learn at school, but I suspect that it was hearing enormous quantities of his chamber music later at Oxford which led me to believe that enough was almost as good as a feast. I had no desire to appear unfashionable. This was a period when Brahms was admired out of all proportion to his real worth and 'Public School' music could be said to be based on a respectable imitation of the manner. All this time my quiet enthusiasm for Bach was maturing.

When Dr Thatcher was away examining for the Associated Board, my piano lessons were given by Leslie Taylor. Once in 1932 he took me to the Temple where I was able to admire Thalben-Ball conducting a choir with his right hand while transposing the *Sanctus* of the B minor Mass down a semitone with his left. Another fine organist heard about this period was Quentin MacLean, who used to make a speciality of including 'good' music in his cinema organ recitals. At this time I won an organ prize at school, wore glasses for the first time and in September enjoyed a holiday with the Iago family on their yacht in the Percuil River near Falmouth.

I have been unlucky with flute-players. Some in a trivial way: those who went on playing when others had stopped, like one I knew in Aberystwyth, and those who froze into silence, like the man in Oxford who stopped playing when scowled at half way through a Gade symphony. Others have been my friends, and two died tragically young. Marcus Holmes, for whom I wrote a duo for two unaccompanied flutes to be played with his wife, died of infantile paralysis soon after the war. My other and older friend was John Iago. Many were the musical occasions — for him I wrote a flute sonata — and the conjuring evenings and games with Meccano and electric trains. When war came John joined the navy. A commission on *HMS Hood* was a long way from the yacht in Falmouth harbour. In May 1941 this battle cruiser was sunk by the *Bismarck* in the northern Atlantic with the loss of 1,400 officers and men. There were only three survivors of this action in which the cruiser blew up after the fifth salvo from the German battleship. I remembered that John had told me that his quarters were just above the magazine, and this was quite probably where the unlucky shot struck which killed the great ship in two minutes, 500 miles north-east of Cape Farewell. Three days later the *Bismarck* was sunk. *"Covered by the same ocean,"* said Ernle Bradford [2], *"they lie deep. The long Atlantic swell will never stir their hulls. Until all the seas run dry, they have no memorial except in the minds of men."* Of John, his aunt, Dora Bowen, wrote [3]:

*"Is it Man's fate ever to spend himself
in vain Crusade?
And are we mocked who seek a lasting peace?
I only know that now you lie so deep
No hurricanes shall rouse you from that sleep."*

IV Royal College of Music

After a typical public school existence, with its emphasis on 'manly' pursuits, in September 1932 I went to the Royal College of Music. Every day I used to go up to Paddington and walk through the park to South Kensington. My first memory is of queuing up for lunch amidst an enormous crowd of young women. Desperately I looked round to see if there were any men in sight — there were a few men students, as it turned out. Through my old friend Norman Strachan, I met John Wray who had been at Bishop's Stortford. Robin Miller altered the colouring of my domestic concertos by his playing the trombone. My main cronies at the time became Deryck Seymour and William Hook, both specialising in the organ as I was. The choir practices were most ably accompanied by Charles Groves, who was also a most cheerful member of the conducting class.[4]

This was the time when I was introduced to the music of Wagner and Bartók. The former's 'magic ban' (or 'sleep') motif in *Walküre* seemed strange enough when it cropped up in Basil Allchin's aural training class, which also contained surprises from Delius and Schoenberg for dictation, but taking to Bartók was like a cold plunge: not an easy or palatable thing to be undertaken, but, like every cold plunge, exhilarating and warming to look back on.

The influence of Sir Percy Buck and his anecdotes was quite lasting, especially the story of the deaf bugler bursting his lungs into his instrument on a desert island and producing no sound. His *The Scope of Music* I liked, just as I enjoyed *The Growth of Music* by H C Colles, whose history lectures were attended, but Buck's *Unfigured Harmony* struck me as an unsatisfactory book because of the curious styleless style which inevitably came from using it and his unwarranted branding of a simple sequence (which Bach would not have spurned) as "inconceivably trite".

Dr Henry Ley took me for organ, and Albert Garcia, grandson of the famous Manuel Garcia, for singing. Dr E T Cook of Southwark took classes on choir training and matters connected with church music, and Professor Kitson gave me theory lessons. From the point of view of getting a scholarship to Oxford on standard harmony and counterpoint, Dr Kitson was superb. With regard to modern music, he admitted he was frankly out of touch. As a result I lived a double life: writing one sort of music (free from consecutives and other scandalous progressions) for my teacher in the daytime and another freely created sort for myself at night.

At the end of my 1932 diary I wrote out the strange figure 142857, which, multiplied by any number up to six, produces the same figures in order in the answer and, when multiplied by seven, makes 999999. Fascinating also was the word square which can be read all ways:

```
R O T A S
O P E R A
T E N E T
A R E P O
S A T O R
```

(The sower Arepo holds the works, namely the wheels.) The letters can be used to make ORO TE PATER, ORO TE PATER, SANAS (We pray, thee, Father, thou healest) and it is an anagram of PATER NOSTERAO.

V 1933

The 1933 diary starts with a few more jokes: Anthem for organist using bad language : 'I said in my haste'—Blow! Books to read : *Appendicitis* by Henrietta Stone, *The Cliff Tragedy* by Eileen Dover, *O Sole Mio* by Phyletta Playce, *Amongst the Lions* by Claude Badley, etc.

On January 12th, the family went to the Albert Hall to hear Paderewski, whose programme was mainly Chopin, and who included about six encores, and on March 9th, Mother and I went to hear Chaliapin, whose acting mannerisms fascinated me.

In March, shortly after my seventeenth birthday, I went to Oxford to sit for the New College Music Scholarship. The examiners were Sir Hugh Allen and Dykes Bower. One of the other candidates was the grandson of Sir John Stainer. I was placed first, but Sir Hugh Allen considered me too young to go up that year, and the scholarship was kept for the next year. About this time I visited the church near Edgware, on the organ of which "Handel composed the divine oratorio *Esther*", according to the plaque, and while staying at our bungalow at Angmering-on-Sea, Sussex, we went on to Littlehampton Congregational Church to hear an organ recital by Master Ivor Keys ARCO, who was only fourteen and was soon to build something of a reputation as a prodigy (on another occasion he was billed as Scout Keys).

On May 9th, a Jubilee Concert was given at the RCM in the presence of the King and Queen. The conductors included Dan Godfrey and Bliss. Sir Hugh conducted three of the *Songs of the Fleet* by Stanford, and I was impressed by Landon Ronald's conducting of Holst's *Jupiter*. The orchestra included, amongst others, R Nicholson, J Whitehead, W Gaskell, E Rothwell [5], J Denison and I Lemare, who were all to become better known. Seymour and Groves were singing bass next to me.

Dr Ley, while instructing me on the use of organ stops, particularly in trio playing, said that he knew the actual horn player who played *The Merry Widow* undetected while Nikisch was conducting Strauss's *Domestic Symphony*. In Mozart every instrument is individual, but the ear today is jaded. When, a few months later, I showed Dr Ley my scherzo for orchestra, he considered it full of beef, a welcome contrast to the 'graveyard music' written today. Dr Buck's elder brother said to him: "Music is meant to be beautiful, therefore why are there any discords in it?" He answered, as he told us in his lecture, that music is not meant to be beautiful but interesting. The beauty is in our reaction to it. When you are young, you like a picture with a pretty face on it, but chocolate boxes have pretty faces on them. He had a picture in his study by Velasquez of an ugly old man with warts all over his face — a fine picture, emotional interest being heightened.

Dr (later Sir George) Dyson gave a lecture on Modern Music which, he said, is written with quick thinking. If you want to understand it, you must be like the pedestrians in London; they are of two kinds, the quick and the dead. Ravel he described as writing in musical telegraphese — putting in all the strong words and leaving out the weak ones. Much later, I was to read the surprisingly penetrating observation of Samuel Butler (*Luck or Cunning?*, 1887): "*Whether a discord is too violent or no depends on what we have been accustomed to, and on how widely the new differs from the old...*".

In my diary I contemplated the phenomenon of taste in the use of words. What might be considered the most beautiful words apply to what I then called "infernal noises": accordion, concertina, harmonium, Musical Comedy, concert party, music hall. What's in a name! The words euphonium and dulcitone are surely better than hautbois or fiddle.

My first full-scale Wagnerian experience was of *Siegfried* at Golders Green conducted by Albert Coates, with Walter Widdop in the name part. It made a profound impression, even though one of the main memories is of admiration for the wonderfully realistic steam which rose when the newly forged blade was plunged into cooling water.

During the year I attended three performances of the B minor Mass.

Among other works, I composed Variations on *The Last Rose of Summer* for flute, trombone, two violins, cello and two pianofortes, containing, besides *The Last Rose* in augmentation, diminution, upside-down, backwards, stretto and whole-tone, the following tunes in combination with it or with themselves: *Old 100th, God Save the King, Lincolnshire Poacher* (in stretto) and *All Creatures of our God and King*. Dr Kitson's laconic comment was "ingenious".

VI Music Scholarship and Germany

More books to read appear at the beginning of my 1934 diary: *Angry Parents* by Margot Crosse, *The Acrobat* by Gideon Wyre, *Beware of the Bull* by Gordon A Horne, *The Deserted Beach* by Baron C Shaw and *Traffic Obstructions* by Edwards Carr, MusBac.

In February I witnessed the lavish pageant performance of *Elijah* conducted by Albert Coates at the Albert Hall, complete with fire descending from heaven, storm and rain thrown on to a screen, ballet, huge chorus and orchestra. I was not too impressed by the fiery chariot.

In my diary I noted the death of Sir Edward Elgar at 8am on February 23rd. At this time, his music had not made a great impression on me, but thanks partly to John Wray, who also obtained a scholarship to Oxford at the same time, my enthusiasm slowly developed. Wray followed the already legendary Joseph Cooper at Keble. Joe Cooper's fame rested at this time on his ability to improvise a fugue on a current dance-tune and to be met after the service with "A little early Bach, I presume?" from an elderly don.

Before going up to Oxford I was translating ten lines of Virgil a day so as to recover some of the Latin which I had lost during the period at the RCM. We had a mademoiselle with the family which helped to brush up the French as well.

On May 25th I noted the death of Gustav Holst, a composer who had made a fair impression on me by this time; and on June 10th that of Delius, whose music I preferred in smaller doses. Since that year, which took three of the greatest composers of our time, I have visited Elgar's birthplace, now a museum, near Worcester, often passed near the plaque in Cheltenham where Holst was born, and actually stayed in Delius's birthplace in Bradford, which became a private hotel.

Two interesting experiences in June were visiting the St Nicolas College of Church Music, then at Chislehurst, where my friends Miller and Mulgan were studying, and attending the Festival of English Church Music at Windsor, where I met Sir Walford Davies — I was to hear much of him later when I went to Wales. Quentin MacLean's playing of Bach's D major Fugue (the Toodleoodle) at the Royal College of Organists is a brilliant memory.

In July we spent a holiday near Minehead. We watched the barley reaping and the rabbits being shot as they rushed out at the end; we saw the church where Lorna Doone was supposed to have been married, and we had a fine ride on ponies along the Doone Valley. Then on to St Ives, where some French sailors in blue clothes and clogs were staying. On the way home we visited Stonehenge and Salisbury Cathedral.

In September Father gave me my first driving lesson, and on October 11th I drove part of the way to Oxford where I was matriculated. My 'moral' tutor was Mr A H Smith, later to be Warden of New College. Early on I had tea with Mrs Bridges, wife of the poet, whose daughter Margaret had been the wife of Mr Joseph, my tutor, who had founded the scholarship in her memory. I took the first B.Mus at the end of my first term. Many of the music scholars of the various colleges became my friends, and I met Humphrey Searle, who was at New College. Denis Mulgan, Worcester, was much in demand as oboist. Other organ scholar friends were Charles Palmer, Wadham, and Kenneth Malcolmson, Exeter. Norman Strachan went up to St Edmund Hall, and his old school friend, John Wray, became organ scholar of Keble.

In the summer of 1935 I had the exciting experience of going to Germany, staying in Munich for the purpose of improving my German and my viola playing as well as for a general education. Also there was wonderful scenery, mountains like the Wendelstein, towns such as Innsbruck, and often music when one got there. Salzburg, for example, with the Mozarteum and, strangely, a 'British' concert with the first performance of Bliss's *Music for Strings*, and the Herreninsel im Chiemsee with its fantastic Versailles-like castle and chamber music under the chandeliers played by the Studeny Quartet (led by the lady from whom I had lessons). I also visited the Hofbräuhaus, as yet a simple beer-hall; and Dachau, then an innocent and picturesque village. There was Wagnerian opera in abundance and also the experience of seeing Richard Strauss and Hans Pfitzner in action as conductors of their own music.

VII Oxford

Some regard Lawrence
With abhorrence
And like Priestley
Who's not beastly
(*The Isis*, October 1936)

In 1936 Saxony was paying approximately £100,000 a year for the maintainance of the Dresden Opera. Twenty years later, after being defeated in the second world war, cities and municipalities in Germany were again supporting their opera houses with lavish grants; yet the position of opera in Britain had sunk so low that there were fewer companies (desperately few in any case) and actually less money for the lucky ones — which could be counted on the thumbs of both hands. In 1936 I did actually see the Carl Rosa Company in action, as well as paying visits to the Garden and the Wells. After the war the Carl Rosa was gradually squeezed out of existence. There were almost no other companies at all, and yet in Germany a town of a few hundred thousands could have its own opera house.

In January 1936, William Hook, known affectionately as 'Hooky', and I went to the Hungarian Prom at the old Queen's Hall. Although Kodály was unable to appear, with the consequence that Sir Henry Wood conducted *Háry János*, we had the memorable experience of hearing Bartók as soloist in his own Piano Concerto No.2, after which he played some short, simple and charming piano pieces, including the *Rondo* on folk tunes in C (which I played four months later myself at Oxford).

This was the month in which King George V died; there was much music-making and listening at Oxford as well as other oddities such as attending an Oxford Group meeting, where the 'confessors' struck me at the time as conceited and boring. Apart from chapel music and distinguished visitors, such as Keith Faulkner, Kipnis, the Kutcher Quartet, the Roth Quartet (playing Bartók No.1), the Griller Quartet, Kathleen Long, Constant Lambert (conducting Liszt for Searle), a good deal of Oxford musical life involved doing it yourself. My viola was frequently in use on a number of chamber music and orchestral occasions. One of these was the Schubert Octet at the Music Club to an audience of "about two". The gramophone, Prince Prem Purachatra's for Siamese music and Dr Watson's for the Walton Symphony, and the wireless, often Denis Mulgan's for Puccini, Berlioz or Berg, were frequently in use, while for outdoor relaxation we skated on Port Meadow, often going through when the ice was too thin, and much tennis — and even at one stage some water polo.

One of my first public performances was of the first *Scherzo*, which I conducted with the 'Isis' Orchestra on February 16th. At a second performance on March 9th it was actually encored, and when it was done again on June 18th, I referred to it as the "inevitable scherzo". Sydney Watson was at this time a broadening influence. His sympathies ranged from Glazunov, who died in March and whose Sixth Symphony had impressed me quite a good deal, to Peter Warlock, soon to make a deeper impression. He played the incidental music to *Macbeth* by Matthew Locke, which caused by its cheerfully naïve disregard for the grimness of the words much hilarity. My diary includes criticisms of Elgar's *The Music Makers* and Bax's Third Symphony, which were not very flattering, but I enjoyed Verdi's *Falstaff* at Sadlers Wells in March. On a second hearing of the Bax, I said: *"Four bars or so may sound impressive, but the whole thing is maddening"*.

In one day in May, I was able to combine attending a performance of *Murder in the Cathedral* with listening to Sir Donald Tovey lecturing in the Sheldonian on 'Normality and Freedom in Music'. A story about Tovey struck me at this time. He arrived one evening before a lecture on Beethoven, and his host noticed that he was muttering. As he went to bed he was observed still to be talking to himself, and when people listened carefully, they discovered that he was talking about Beethoven. The next morning at breakfast he was still talking about Beethoven. On the way to the Sheldonian he was still muttering, and when he went up on to the platform to give the address, he *went on* talking about Beethoven. On May 28th my diary recounts that I *"saw one of the very worst films that I have ever seen — 'A Midsummernight's Dream'. All the players assumed that Shakespeare was nonsense anyway and had to be redeemed by maniacal noises or hearty American accents. James Cagney was an extraordinarily bad Bottom and Mickey Rooney was a horrible Puck. Everything was disgusting, including the dishing up of Mendelssohn's music. As Prem said, ' It was best when they didn't drag Shakespeare into it', but I think he was too indulgent."*

After passing the second examination for the B.Mus, I went at the end of term to stay with the Crums in the precincts of Canterbury Cathedral. This included seeing the 'Red' Dean (without politics) and visiting the bells and the organ, as well as a Holst Memorial Concert in the cloisters with a *"long and very unpoetical speech on the composer by Masefield, mentioning his fondness for onions and bitter beer"*, the music being mainly choral pieces of a subdued nature. Afer this I went to the St Nicolas College of Church Music at Chislehurst, meeting a blind student called Lewis Jones, who had been up at Balliol about ten years previously, whom I was not to see again for about twenty years. The activities ranged from plainsong to folk-dancing, but the pleasant interchange of ideas was as important as anything, and I improved my organ playing sufficiently to take and pass the ARCO. This was followed by a holiday at Chagford, with tramping and riding over Dartmoor with Deryck Seymour. We did some sketching at Widecombe and rode to where the Dart and Teign rise — it *"were terrible boggy an' all"*. On August 6th the family went to Portsmouth for part of Navy Week, and we had tea on *HMS Hood*. Four days later we saw the H G Wells film, *Things to Come*.

In September I visited the Three Choirs Festival at Hereford, where I found *Gerontius* less satisfying than *The Apostles* or *The Kingdom*. The influence of Wagner is unfortunately of the immature *Tannhäuser* period; it intrudes in the later oratorios but not so objectionably as in 'The Dream'. Dyson's *Nebuchadnezzar* is a fabricated piece of sensation ... a poor effort for a man who could write a book like *The New Music?*

Cecil Gray's book on Warlock is described as a very unsuccessful defence of drunkenness, poor GBS being attacked for his sobriety. At the same time I was studying Aldous Huxley's caricature of Warlock in *Antic Hay*. The Markova Ballet performed at Oxford in October, including *David* by Maurice Jacobson.

Throughout the years at Oxford, Sir Hugh Allen was a kindly, thoughtful father to the music students; he meant much more to us than did any of the other members of staff. When Dr Armstrong had mumps in January 1937, Sir Hugh took the Bach choir. He gave us the full impact of his vital energetic personality and passed on his terrific enthusiasm for the Beethoven Mass in D. My swimming friend, Rigby, aptly described him as "dynamite". My regular friends and contemporaries at New College were J Richardson (died 1984), H Huggill, M Crum, F Nabarro (who went to South Africa) and L Walker.

On November 15th, the Vice-Chancellor in his sermon in our chapel talked of healthy irreverence and that making fun of things that people take too seriously was a good thing. This fortified me considerably before the Balliol Concert, at which Denis Mulgan gave a magnificent performance of my Oboe Sonata. The last movement, which is a deliberately surrealist pastiche, was well received in the right spirit by the audience who called me back twice, though I felt that the generations of dons in the portraits round the walls were frowning down.

In December of the year in which his father had died, King Edward VIII abdicated and became the Duke of Windsor.

VIII 1937

1937 was a year, the first in which Oxford had won the Boat Race for fourteen years, in which I took part, in the chorus, in a television performance of Blow's *Venus and Adonis* after it had first been done at Oxford. It was an interesting experience at that time to be at Alexandra Palace, feeling the great lamps beating down on us. I had remembered Neville Coghill, the producer, say to the huntsmen about to embrace the shepherdesses: "Kiss her! Don't peck like the vultures at Prometheus's guts".

Under the encouragement of Mr Harold Spicer, organist of Manchester College, I had some teaching practice at a school quite near, which was decidedly useful for one who was still primarily introspective.

Chief guests at my 21st birthday party were my mother and father, 'uncle' Teddy Biggs, uncle Hugh and aunt Dorothy, and aunt Sallie. A performance of *Turandot* at Covent Garden in May was memorable for Eva Turner and Barbirolli; Smeterlin was the outstanding pianist I heard at Oxford in the year.

Humphrey Searle wrote to Cecil Gray, and we hoped that he would come to my Peter Warlock concert. Cecil Gray pointed out that a string accompaniment would be quite in order to support the singers in the *Dirges*, so we duly organised the Kirby String Quartet, muted. Neither Gray nor Sir Richard Terry were eventually able to attend on May 30th, when I conducted a concert at St Hugh's of Music by Peter Warlock. The soloists were Winifred Dussek, F Wade and E Manning. Denis Mulgan and Robin Miller assisted at the piano in *The Lady's Birthday*, and for *The Curlew* the cor anglais was played by Elizabeth Kitson.

On the following day I attended a debate between Bertrand Russell and Sir Norman Angell. Their aim was peace: only their methods differed. The one was by pacifism, the other by collective security. Both successfully destroyed each other's policy, I wrote at the time, and I thought that the result seemed that both policies were hopeless.

For the last time, I went down from Oxford in June with BA and B.Mus, and although offered a job at Felsted, took the post of assistant director of music at Malvern College.

David Cox (died 1996), who came over from Australia and whom I first met at St Nicolas College in 1936, won a composition scholarship to the RCM. He came to see us in Harrow, and we exchanged ideas on composition. 'Hooky' (died 1993) and I had a smooth crossing from Newhaven to Dieppe in September and joined Norman Strachan in Paris for a holiday which included *Femmes Savantes*, *Malade Imaginaire*, visits to Exhibition, Eiffel Tower, Notre Dame, Versailles, the Louvre, and a very poor opera by Ibert called *L'Aiglon* followed by a good one, *Ariadne auf Naxos* by Richard Strauss. We also enjoyed the coffee, cognac and cigars.

On September 22nd, I got out of the train at Malvern and took a horse-cab to my new digs. These were comfortable but, as there was no bath, I used to swim in the College baths at 7.15am on most mornings. My retired predecessor lived at Forli, Alexandra Road, where Elgar had worked on *Gerontius*. I also met Dr Hamand, the organist of the Priory Church, and much liked his company.

In November I went over to Oxford for one of the Waterhouse's Cantata Parties. My diary scarcely does justice to one of the items: "...*A solo from another cantata was sung with Ursula's obbligato on the flute...*". It may seem strange today, but it was on one of these delightful occasions just south of Oxford, that I was so entranced by a soprano singing with two flutes and piano that I asked to see the music. It appeared that the music could only be obtained in Germany, so I set to work to copy it out. I then cherished this lovely music and did no more than play it and think about it from time to time. Within a few years other, and perhaps harder, heads than mine had done more than consider copying it. They had sent it to publishers, and it appeared in so many guises — the first I believe was for two pianos — that it would be difficult to count them all. This quiet little secular aria, at that time virtually unknown, was called *Schafe können sicher weiden*. I might have made a lot of money out of *Sheep May Safely Graze*.

IX Malvern

My total income in 1938 was £170.15, and I imagine this was the first time I had earned anything. Teaching music at a public school was considered a good job in those days, and many of my contemporaries continued in that occupation, which they found congenial. My tendency, however, was to prefer being 'up in the air' to being 'down to earth'.

A certain interest in surrealism over the last few years, including reading André Breton and Cocteau, as well as writing that somewhat eccentric finale to the Oboe Sonata, was to have a curious testing. My cousin, Nindi Clarke, was desperately ill in 1938, and I remember how I stood silently in awe by her bed listening to the strange apparently unconnected words flowing from her lips. Later, when reading Dylan Thomas, I was to think again that the unchecked outpourings of genius often resemble those of the sick mind. My cousin wanted me to play the piano, and she said: "Play something — not too thundery — I like something played on the lawn". There was much more, of course, of a similar nature.

Up to this time, it had all been just amusing or irritating in 'modern' poetry. I had played myself with 'joycy' and 'juicy' and said: "'You have plenty of *savoir-faire*' sang Freud". My general contempt for 'clever' verse was expressed by such lines as :

> *"Wait.*
>   *Wait until.*
>   *Wait until the.*
>   *To stop the train*
>   *Pull down the chain*
>   *So early in the morning."*

and

> *"In*
> *The city of lost horses and dreaming choirs,*
> *How odd of God to build the Bod.*
> *While dagdalen over Magdalen*
> *He moucester missed Worcester."*

Looking back on it, it seems that despite the enthusiasm for surrealism, the shade of W S Gilbert was leaning over my shoulder. However, I copied out a good deal from, mainly, French authors on this fashionable subject. *"Reality"*, said Breton, *"is the dandelion blown by the woman who appears on the front page of dictionaries"*. Strangely, concurrently I was copying, mainly from German authors, a good deal of psychoanalysis, also fashionable then. The authors included Freud, Adler, Dreikurs, Halliday Sutherland, MacDougall King, etc. Shortly I was to switch to psychical research, finding that all this psychoanalysis was not about the mind as I had hoped but more about behaviour. I was also being gently persuaded one way to read *First Aid to the Injured* and *ARP* (having joined St John's Ambulance and enlisted as a special constable) and then jostled the other way to read *Encyclopaedia of Pacifism* edited by Aldous Huxley; and such titles as *Why Spain Fights On* and *Red Star Over China*. At one stage I actually left an *Elijah* rehearsal to go through a gas van — not that I could ever share the enthusiasm of John Davison, the director of music, for that oratorio.

In January Denis Mulgan and I heard the first performance in England, conducted by Scherchen, of *Music for Strings, Percussion and Celesta*, of which I had just obtained the score. This was really something memorable which profoundly affected me as a composer. Musical entertainments such as this were more important to me than all the other 'unreal' influences, though I was at the time somewhat impressed by a young poet called Basil Hembrey — later to leave London and settle down as a farmer in Devonshire.

One way of describing my visit to Dr Armstrong Gibbs is to quote from his address given a couple of months later on Friday March 25th 1938 [6]:

> *"Will our successors a century hence find Schönberg and Bartók as intelligible as we now find Beethoven?*
>
> *Quite possibly, but I'm by no means certain.*
>
> *In this connection I have recently had an interesting experience: a young man whom I had not then met, but who had a connection through friends and relations, sent me a work for piano for my opinion.*

After looking it over and playing it through several times, I decided there was much of it that appeared to me quite hideous. The form and scheme were clear enough and perfectly logical. It was the sound that I couldn't stomach. I wrote to him and criticised it to this effect. I further said it struck me like a sentence in which the grammar was faultless but the words meaningless, such as "it behoves us to incinerate whether the ant-eaters televise their incisors", and that it sounded entirely cerebral and unemotional.

It was, too, very strongly influenced by Bartók.

I was somewhat surprised to receive a charming and most humble-minded letter from him in which he said among other things that he was sorry that I regarded his music as "cerebral" as it had in point of fact been written to express a very poignant and personal emotional experience. The letter was so obviously sincere that I asked him to come and see me, which he did. I got him to play his work several times and while I still could not appreciate it, I was left with no doubt as to his complete sincerity. He discussed polytonality at some length and when I said that I could see his point logically but that my ear could not accept his logic he quite flattened me by remarking "Of course I have been careful to choose only such combinations of keys as sound grateful to the ear". This I felt was a proof of my middle age with a vengeance."

Later that year Humphrey Searle and I exchanged letters to *The Musical Times* on the subject of polytonality. The split in attitudes was becoming more acute; at least Searle and I were arguing about different *modern* tendencies, but there were people like Armstrong Gibbs saying my music, still immature though it was, was "too modern", when Sorabji had just said the same piece was "not modern enough"!

After joining the Worcester orchestra, I was bold enough to show this same piece to Sir Ivor Atkins, but without response. In March I met the architect Troyte Griffith. He had mellowed considerably, I would say, since the variation, 'Troyte', was written. Then in April I saw *Gianni Schicchi* for the third time and remarked that it does not lose its charm. We saw many films, and it seemed that only in French films did the music play a significant artistic part, e.g. Honegger's for *Mayerling*. Then the family stayed at Duncton, visiting Petworth House (with the Grinling Gibbons room which took four years to carve), and Pulborough, where

Denis and Julia Mulgan and I joined Mr Richard Border in his studio for Purcell, Denis and I taking it in turns to play either piano or viola, surrounded by Mr Border's innumerable and invaluable autographs and first editions.

For the Three Choirs Fesival in 1938 I met Lennox Berkeley at the Atkins's and became interested in his music. He conducted his *Domini est Terra*, which was quite an innovation for Worcester in those days, and I met him in London again later in the year when he encouraged me as a composer.

Notes to Part One
- [1] Capt William MacDowall, RN, who died in 1867, my grandmother's father, was the son of a man who was said to have married Tipoo Sahib's youngest daughter.
- [2] *The Mighty Hood* [Hodder & Stoughton, 1959]
- [3] *The Radnor Hills & Other Poems* [Wilding, Shrewsbury, 1955]
- [4] Sir Charles Groves died, aged 77, in June 1992.
- [5] As fellow Vice-Presidents, Lady Barbirolli and I shared the Elgar Society Jubilee in September 2001.
- [6] From *The Trend of Modern Music* by C Armstrong Gibbs, MusD, Hon ARCM, published in the Proceedings of the Royal Institution, Volume 30, Part 2, No.141.

Part Two — Love and War

I *Old Tithe Barn*

Life in 1939 started off much as before. The distribution of gas-masks did not interrupt the tennis parties, the listening to Toscanini or even the visit to Glyndebourne (where Denis Mulgan was on the staff and in the stage band for *Figaro*) and writing an opera of my own — not finished.

Something really important happened on August 5th when the family went down to the Old Tithe Barn, North Lancing. Another family had chosen this same place advertised as 'the guest-house of your dreams'. This was Mr & Mrs Edwin Cox and their daughter Elizabeth from Bromley, Kent. Just before their fortnight was up, Elizabeth and I painted Sompting Church together.

Two dramatic events followed.

One was for the whole world; the other was all-important to me. On September 3rd war was declared, and on September 6th I gave Elizabeth a ring. My diary thins out, but this must have been because my heart was beginning to fill. While travelling across London to give my future wife the token of our engagement, the air raid sirens wailed for the first time and, with many other bewildered people, I was herded down below Charing Cross Station. In spite of this, the war scarcely touched London during that momentous month of September.

Barely had I got to know Elizabeth's gentle, gracious mother, when she was taken from us, dying in hospital on September 14th. Elizabeth Parrott was born in Koslov, south Russia. Her father, from Liverpool, had worked for the Union Cold Storage Company in China and South

America before going to Russia where he married Olga Ilinsky. When Mrs Parrott was born, he had to carry the reluctant midwife through Red and White fighting soldiers, later getting his family out to Finland in a cattle truck.

The guiding hand of destiny must have led both Elizabeth's parents and mine to choose the Old Tithe Barn for their holiday. We had none of us been there before, though my family had spent many holidays in Sussex, particularly on the coast further west.

It was a whirlwind engagement, the great happiness being challenged by the terrifying uncertainty of war but never mastered by it. Elizabeth copied out the words of Psalm 91, and I carried them with me wherever I went. When, in 1945, those unforgettable years of never knowing what lay in store had given way to a prospect of peace, I built up a composition, using sketches made at various times during the war, for chorus and orchestra on this *Psalm 91*. The full score was finished in 1947. We were married at Bromley Parish Church on June 1st 1940, just before call-up. Two weekends were all we had for a honeymoon, the first being at Westerham. In my rhapsody for piano of this name, I tried to paint in sound both love and war.

In December 1940 we managed to visit Oxford together and, in order to sit the examinations for the D.Mus, I wore a gown over my battle-dress — a somewhat unusual rig-out. Elizabeth had followed me wherever I was posted, and during the training as an officer-cadet in Aldershot we got to know Bernard Robinson in Farnborough. The work I conducted with his orchestra, in July 1941, was called *A Dream* because the main theme had come to me in a dream the previous year. It was used later as the first subject of a Symphony completed in 1946.

OXFORD UNIVERSITY GAZETTE   4 DECEMBER 1940

DEGREES IN MUSIC
MICHAELMAS TERM, 1940
Names of candidates who have satisfied the Examiners

Examination for the Degree of Doctor of Music
Hely-Hutchinson, Christian Victor Noel Hope, Balliol College
Parrott, Horace Ian, New College

Exercise for the Degree of Bachelor of Music
Bush, Geoffrey, Balliol College
Cox, David Vassall, Worcester College
Gerdin, Leigh, Lincoln College.

First Examination for the Degree of Bachelor of Music
Bullivant, Roger Francis Taylor, New College
Crossley-Holland, Peter Charles, St. John's College
Leeson, Philip Norman, Keble College
Smallman, Frederic Basil Rowley, New College
Vickers, Michael Kenneth, New College

H. P. ALLEN
E. WALKER   } *Examiner.*
W. H. HARRIS

Oxford University Gazette, December 4th 1940

II Overseas

My first posting was to South Eastern Command, during the defeat of Dunkirk, after which Hitler launched a sudden attack on the Soviet Union. Two memories stand out: a meeting of officers convened by the General Officer Commanding, the as yet not well known Bernard Montgomery, who said: "We can consider the Russian Campaign over and must now prepare for invasion" — he was wrong, as it turned out, but at least practical. The other memory is of a big 'Exercise' in which I was the Signal Master at Divisional HQ, when a plane dropped a message which landed in a very tall tree. I reported this to the fearsome CO, who barked at me: "Climb the tree". Since it was clearly impossible, I was emboldened to reply: "I challenge you to climb it — sir". After that, the matter was dropped, though the message wasn't.

It wasn't long before I was part of a draft crammed into a converted luxury liner which was in convoy to an 'unknown' destination — with the German warships, *Scharnhorst, Gneisenau* and *Prinz Eugen,* managing to miss us in the Atlantic. After changing ships at Durban — with a three-week break — we knew we were for the Middle East. Another draft was lucky to be diverted from Singapore, which had just fallen to the Japanese. In Durban my latest song, written at sea, was sung by Doreen Rasmussen, and I was given the chance to conduct the local orchestra. As I couldn't get leave from Amanzimtoti camp for a rehearsal, it was somewhat touch-and-go, standing in the wings to be told that I'd find the cellos "on the left". When I faced the band, I found them on the right — and only two of them: not very good for the chosen *William Tell* overture, which starts with divided cellos! However, all was cued in the usual theatre orchestra way, so all was well after all.

On arrival at Suez we were packed into trains for Cairo. When we put our heads out of the openings which served for windows, it felt hotter than inside. It was not much consolation to be told that the *khamseen* was blowing like an oven full of sand.

An Egyptian family called Zaidan was most hospitable to soldiers in the base camp at Mahdi, and I was given a chance to develop a musical association with them and their relations, which included Salma Diab, a composer, and Gina Bachauer — who was later to be a renowned solo pianist.

III Egypt

When the 'high ups' discovered that I had studied German, it was decided that I should go into 'Signals Intelligence'. The base for this was in another Cairo suburb, Heliopolis, reached by a tram-cum-suburban railway. A special pleasure was playing piano duets with Emily (Amy) Anderson, later to be famous as translator of Mozart letters and as the only person who could read Beethoven's handwriting. Then she was employed on Italian ciphers.

Some of us were sent up the desert to a faceless position called Bagush, where it was possible to take a dip from time to time in the warm Mediterranean sea. Since we had access to a priority air bag, there were occasions when I received portions of the libretto of a burlesque opera, *The Sergeant-Major's Daughter*, by this means. After a lot of enthusiastic work by many friends, performances were given at Heliopolis, Helmieh and, finally, at 'Music for All' in Cairo in 1943. This was despite such hazards as having the leading tenor posted to India the day before a performance!

Later I was in a mobile unit called SWG (Special Wireless Group) which swanned around in the desert, owing allegiance only to Army Headquarters. This, when the Germans had made their final advance, was not far from the Delta, at Burg el Arab. Things were at a very low ebb, when you consider that the enemy was winning in every theatre of war. We had picked up an Italian machine gun (Bréda), and I was sent back to an ordnance depot at Alexandria to obtain some ammunition. A very heartening sight met my eyes on my return. Some railway lines ran towards the desert, and on top of some trucks were new tanks, which rolled off westward under their own power. This was coupled with a visit from Churchill with a gradual build-up of resources following. When we heard that Monty was the new Eighth Army commander, I for one felt encouraged.

The adjutant and I both had a spell of leave at a somewhat odd time, because we were in Luxor when the imminence of the Battle of El Alamein brought us back again. But I had already been inspired by the great temples on the east bank and by the tombs of the pharaohs on the west. The result, later, was my symphonic impression, *Luxor* (see next chapter).

The enemy's withdrawal was so quick and unexpected that their dead were left behind unattended and bloated in the hot sun. My first awareness was of the stench. Our follow-up was so fast that we too ignored the bodies — a strange experience. In Cyrenaica we had to 'cut off the corner' by using vast tracts of desert to the south. Halting for a while, I had to find a new alternator, so called on an RAF unit which was nearby. The officer I approached turned out to be James Robertson, a musician! He was later to be the Director of the London Opera Centre. A member of the Board of Trinity College of Music, he toured Australia and New Zealand and conducted the NZ Opera Company in 1969. [1]

When the Eighth Army was rounding the Gulf of Sirte, I had to go out to find our 'forward' unit, consisting of corporal, wireless operator and driver, whose truck had blown up on a mine. It should be explained that the 'special' work we did was not expected to take us too far forward. The 'high ups' would not be very concerned for *our* personal safety, but they would not wish the secret documents we carried to fall into enemy hands. This was a part of the desert where finding out where we were was not particularly easy either, especially when it is realised that the British-style maps of Egypt did not fit neatly into the Italian ones of Libya. Somehow we found our way back to our companions, even though the whole army was constantly on the move.

By the New Year, we found ourselves near the Roman amphitheatre of Leptis Magna, well worth a visit under more congenial circumstances, and I found time to write another song, this time called *Absence*. It was during this period that I was able to check that my enthusiasm for the extrasensory did not over-ride my commonsense. It was quite usual to be sleeping in a hole in the sand when some bombs were dropped fairly near, and three times I woke up in advance of the explosion. Precognition? No, it was the fact that sound travels faster through sand than through air. So, in a way I experienced the same sound twice!

When we reached Tripoli, some of us had an incongruous experience. We went into a left-over hotel carrying our bully beef and tinned fish. Italian waiters served us with wine as we ate our rations with our fingers.

I was then given the job of escorting some of our vehicles and equipment back to Cairo. On the road pocked with mine holes we took about nine days for the thousand miles to the Delta. I was told that, in peacetime, an Italian racing driver had done it in nine *hours*.

Shortly afterwards I was transferred to GSI Top (Topographical) as a signals 'expert'. In so far as I knew slightly more about signals communications, including peacetime submarine cables in Greece, than the mapmakers, it was partly true. The submarine cables were mostly out of action, and it soon became clear that what secrecy the Germans could preserve was now due to the invention of radar. As is now well known, this proved to be of great importance to both sides, as the war progressed.

At one time I lived in a flat in Cairo. When my very old friend, Norman Strachan, came to join John (Bobby) Runge and myself, he lived 'upstairs', the Arabic word being foq. So Abdu, our servant, called him Mr Foq, "because he live-a foq". Fresh water was kept in old gin bottles. One morning Abdu's assistant, the 'foolaboy', made our coffee out of a new bottle. You should have seen our faces as Norman and I gulped neat gin for our breakfast!

When I received a notice that I was to be transferred to the War Office in London, I was so excited that I rushed into the wrong room, disturbing a number of senior New Zealand officers. I also gave a bigger than usual donation to one of the beggars, who sprawled over the pavements of Cairo, as they so often did in a ritualised parody of lamenting.

Notes to Part Two

[1]   Harold Rutland: *Trinity College of Music: the first hundred years* [TCM, London, 1972]

Part Three — The Academic Life

I Aberystwyth

Elizabeth had fitted out a new home for when I got back. It was in Pinner, not so far from my parents in Harrow. Michael (born 1941), who'd not yet met me, greeted me happily with "Hello, Daddy".

Even before I was demobbed, I paced the streets of London looking for a job in music. This turned out first to be taken on as an examiner in music at Trinity College of Music. I remember 'standardising' with Alec Rowley and Edgar Moy while still in uniform. The very lively and efficient Principal was Dr Wilfred Greenhouse Allt. Some years later there was a master of ceremonies who announced in a big voice: "Pray silence for Dr Wilfred Greenhouse —*pause*— *(as if it were a musical diploma)* ALLT". I carried on with the examining business for many years, undertaking two round-the-world tours in 1960 (see article *Globetrotting*, Appendix 1b) and 1970, getting through many thousands of candidates in all grades from tiny tots to adults taking higher diplomas.

We all moved to Birmingham in 1946 for three happy years while I was lecturer in music in the University Music Department, the professor being Anthony Lewis. It was during this time that I received the honour of First Prize of the Royal Philharmonic Society for my symphonic impression, *Luxor*. Its first performance was with the LPO under Sir Adrian Boult in London and Oxford in 1950.

1950 was the year in which I was appointed Gregynog Professor of Music in the University College of Wales, Aberystwyth. I wrote of my 33 years in the chair in the magazine *Welsh Music* (see article *Thirty-three Years in Welsh Music*, Appendix 1c).

II The Guild for the Promotion of Welsh Music

Soon after out move to Aberystwyth, I was persuaded by the energetic John Edwards to become a founder member of the GPWM, and in those early days I believe we really put on events of value. Apart from the annual congresses, in which the BBC Welsh Orchestra, inspired by Mansel Thomas and conducted by Arwel Hughes, took part, we managed two important competitions. The first for pianists in 1959 was widely advertised throughout the whole country, and I found myself one of the adjudicators for a preliminary round in Liverpool. I remember waiting for the next candidate when the doorman produced a scruffy piece of paper on which was written: "Mr Ogdon as withdrawd". At that time, John Ogdon was virtually unknown, but if he'd stayed in our competition, I don't doubt that he may well have won. As it was, he went on from strength to strength, within three years becoming joint winner with Ashkenazy of the Tchaikovsky Prize.

Our finals were held in Cardiff in November, and the hundred guinea prize was won by Ivan Quinnell, a record being made of his playing. What made our competition particularly interesting was that a contemporary Welsh work was required. This was David Wynne's Sonata No.1, which, in spite of its difficulty, did not deter more than 80 competitors.

Ian and Elizabeth with Ming, Penglais Road, Aberystwyth, 1950s

The second competition, held in 1966, was for violinists. It also required the performance of an exacting modern composition: David Harries's Violin Concerto. [1]

As a member of Council of the Incorporated Society of Musicians, I was able to persuade our President, Yehudi Menuhin, to take on the position of chief adjudicator. With his characteristic generosity he gave his services for nothing.

After the routine of preliminary rounds, six finalists appeared in the Reardon Smith Lecture Theatre, Cardiff, on July 2nd 1966. Sadly, John Edwards did not live to enjoy the fruits of his labours. He had died in May that year.

The prizes included an engagement to broadcast the Harries Concerto with the BBC Welsh Orchestra. At a later stage I was persuaded to interview the three finalists for a position on my staff in the Music Department at UCW Aberystwyth, and so one was appointed. Although a good violinist in his way, he didn't prove very helpful in the department, preferring his own activities. After I had retired, he found it equally difficult to get on with my successor, so presented himself to the Principal. It was said that he imagined himself to be indispensable, but the Principal, more interested in 'rationalisation', gladly accepted his resignation.

Being something of a G&S enthusiast, I cannot resist the temptation to insert a *Gondoliers* parody, as follows (to be sung to the tune of the Duke of Plaza-Toro):

> *In enterprize with music men*
> *When there was College music,*
> *He led his instruments from behind —*
> *He found it less obtrusive.*
> *But when outside his orchestra played,*
> *His place was at the fore, O—,*
> *That most affected*
> *Undetected*
> *Well-protected fiddle-d-dee,*
> *The Duke of Robert-Boro.*
> *When told that they would all be sacked*
> *Unless they left the service,*
> *That hero hesitated not.*
> *So marvellous his nerve is.*
> *He sent his resignation in,*
> *The finest of all his corps, O!*
> *That very wearing*

> *Over-bearing*
> *Not endearing Violin*
> *The Duke of Robert-Boro.*
>
> Anon after WSG

After John Edwards' death we instituted an annual award for an outstanding Welsh musician or organisation. The first of these in 1967 was made to Alun Hoddinott. It was followed by an award the next year to Glynne Jones and the Pendyrus Male Voice Choir. Then it was back to a composer: Grace Williams in 1969. When Sir Geraint Evans became president the next year, the presentations were made annually by him for more than twenty years. He died on September 19th 1992, but the awards continue.

I enjoyed my time as vice-chairman, frequently being called on by Glanville Jones, the lawyer chairman, to make a speech or a presentation at the drop of a hat. One occasion I remember was when I told Daniel Jones that I'd recently been talking to a musician in London (Dr Bill Pasfield) who was a fan of his music. With a great shout, Dan replied: "So I have a *fan*?" When I went on to present him to Sir Geraint for the award in 1987, I was tactless enough to say that he was the twenty-second recipient. His characteristic comment, again with a shout, was: "So there were twenty-one people considered better than me, were there?!" Knowing his aptness for the unexpected, we took this, of course, as an example of his individual sense of fun. He was, in fact, an extremely imaginative and erudite musician, and he sent me a most informative letter when I was writing about Peter Warlock. This, in March 1993, only a month before his death, gave me details not only of Arbeau's *Orchésographie* in the British Museum Catalogue, but also about his friend, Dylan Thomas, and the poet Victor Neuburg, which I needed as Neuburg was in fact also in the Warlock story. [2]

III Postlude

Elizabeth had shared my interest in Elgar, her picture of Brinkwells, the cottage in Sussex, appearing on an EMI record sleeve. She had been instrumental in having the thatch preserved in the place where he wrote the late chamber music.

Sadly, four years after we had celebrated our Golden Wedding in 1990, Elizabeth passed away. At Llanbadarn Church, where in 1985 she had initiated the installation and dedication of a John Petts window, a service on October 24th 1994 was attended by a large congregation of those from far and near who had loved her.

The Ancient Church of Llanbadarn by Elizabeth Parrott

I am not quite sure whether these lines of Masefield expressed what I felt:

> *I held that when a person dies*
> *His soul returns again to earth;*
> *Arrayed in some new flesh-disguise*
> *Another mother gives him birth.*
> *With sturdier limbs and brighter brain*
> *The old soul takes the road again ...*

These words, however, formed part of the *Songs of Renewal*, performed for the first time at my 80th birthday concert on March 5th 1996. It was dedicated to Jeanne Peckham, whom I married on June 8th that year. Many happy years followed with trips to Madrid, the Rhine and St Petersburg (the last one known to Elizabeth in very different times). I continued with my illustrated lectures on Elgar, Warlock and Cyril Scott, etc, and there was plenty of composition.

There are also occasionally compositions which didn't come about. Quite recently I was recollecting that about sixty years previously I'd read Stefan Zweig's *Die Unsichtbare Sammlung* (*The Invisible Collection*). I thought it would make a fine short opera. It is about a totally blind painter who gets his family to put his collected pictures on show for him, bringing them before him in turn. During the big Depression they fell on hard times, so decide to sell them. After a while they are passing blank canvases before him, pretending to answer his questions and comments. A subject for a young composer?

Being aware that, in my time, a 'serious' composer would sometimes get a 'First Performance' and then be forgotten, I can recall a pleasant experience in July 1993. I had been commissioned by the Parrett (*sic*) Festival to write a piece — the *Fanfare Overture* — given at Montacute on July 3rd by the Southampton Youth Orchestra, conducted by Keith Smith and introduced by the Rt Hon Paddy Ashdown MP (the Leader of the Liberal Democrats). I then had the unprecedented experience of *four* performances within the one week! This was because, before returning to Somerset for another performance there, the Southampton players took part in a gathering of youth orchestras at the Royal Festival Hall. When they had finished, it was announced that the next youth orchestra would be delayed (later it was said that the piccolo player had got stuck in the lift), so the Southampton Orchestra were asked to provide an encore — and guess what! It doesn't often happen to what is now called a 'classical' composer. In my young days, by the way, 'classical' meant strictly of an earlier time, not of one still alive. This piece is now on a CD called 'Welsh Classical Favourites'.

I have also often marvelled at the amount of misunderstanding which arose from Darwin, mostly, I think, from his use of the word 'origin'.

Son, Michael, and Ian with Paddy Ashdown at Montacute, July 3 1993

More interesting to me has been the contemplation of growing and changing languages. Modern American, rather like French and Irish, writes large numbers of letters which are not heard in speech. Take the letter 't'; either it is left out, as in 'Clin'on', 'hun'ing', etc, or it is converted into a 'd', as in 'wriding' and 'nod ad all' and 'led's ged ouda here' etc. Didn't something like this happen when late Latin gradually changed? A millennium ago the Romans' *'amicus'* (friend) became *'amico'* in Italian, but *'amigo'* in Spanish. The 'c' has become 'g', just as now the 't' is becoming 'd'. The French seem to be even lazier; *'ami'* doesn't have an ending at all.

I recollect also how I first learnt about what translation is all about when first I had to study Latin. As youngsters at Orley Farm Prep School we struggled with Caesar's *Gallic Wars*; the opening of one chapter was "*Palus erat non magna*", which, being of a tender age, I dealt with literally, so it came out as "A marsh was not great". It took an enlightened master to talk to me. "Imagine you were writing of your campaign", he said, "and you are introducing a new chapter. Wouldn't you start with something like 'There was a marsh in that place of no great size' or something like that?" That little incident stuck with me, as did two others. Many years later I found myself trying to get to the heart of St Paul's "*Videmus nunc per speculum in aenigmate*". This, although originally in Greek, was heard by Elgar in Latin in the Vulgate version of 1 Cor xiii 12 on Quinquagesima Sunday, February 12th 1899. It was important to me, when writing the Master Musicians *Elgar* in 1971, that I should be able to get to the heart of why Elgar chose to add the word 'enigma' to the score of his *Variations* later in 1899. The well known almost hackneyed 'seeing through a glass darkly' seemed totally inadequate to describe the situation. So, after reading through more than a dozen different versions, including Luther in German, I hit upon J B Phillips's of 1960: "*At present we are men looking at puzzling reflections in a mirror. The time will come when we shall see reality whole and face to face*". For a composer who had changed from a provincial nobody into a world-famous composer, but was too diffident to shout about it, this seemed to me to be the real interpretation.

One more example I have in mind is of a translation which goes further than merely dealing with words. I even had to go against the experts. When I was writing my book, *Cyril Scott and His Piano Music*, in 1992, I wanted to quote from the rather obscure eccentric German poet, Stefan George. Knowing something of the 'spiritualist' world entered by Cyril Scott under the influence of George, I had no hesitation in using the word 'Divine', although the word *'heiligen'* might have been rendered as 'holy'. Therefore the line from *Entrueckung* (*Enraptured*) — "*Ich bin ein funke nur vom heiligen feuer*" — comes out in a translation of its intended meaning as: "*I am but a spark from the Divine fire*".

So, thinking in threes, I might conclude with a contemplation of three basic features of the Christian religion which have impressed me, and then of three writers who similarly have made a lasting impression. The three features are bread, wine and candles; the three writers are Aquinas, Maeterlinck and Dorothy Sayers.

In these days of going to the supermarket for bread and the pub for alcohol, with a switched-on electric light, it should be obvious that two thousand years ago when most food was utterly natural, these three elements needed a living agent to bring them into being, and people marvelled.

Similarly in these days when scientists spend a great deal of time telling us how clever they are, should we not think instead of Aquinas? [3] For example, milk is partly dependent (or contingent) on the cow; the cow is partly dependent on the grass; the grass grows partly because of the sunlight; the sun is partly dependent on hydrogen atoms; the hydrogen atoms ... But it doesn't matter how far you go in your reasoning. It is when *you* stop, there is God.

Then there are problems and mysteries. The former are solvable; the latter not. Take gravity, which has been 'explained' by Newton and others. But Maeterlinck wrote: *"Gravitation is impalpable, invisible, formless, without colour, without odour, without temperature, and silent as thought"*. [4]

Finally Dorothy Sayers. Not the detective thriller writer but the theologian [5]. She applied the doctrine of the Trinity to ordinary human artistic creation. Although she was thinking of the creation of characters in a play, the author being outside the 'book', her ideas can be applied to music. So, for example, it can be said that Bach's aria, *Bist du bei mir*, must once have existed in *his* head. It must also take place with singer and accompanist in performance. Then you go home, saying what a wonderful aria it is. It is now in *your* head. But not three arias. Only one. That is to say: the idea, the expression of the idea, and the impact of the idea. All must be involved for its existence. The difference between artistic creation and Divine Creation is that there will be imperfections in what the human creator does.

While the twentieth century has been moving inexorably into the twenty-first, I've received much encouragement as a composer from many people: Capt and Mrs Lambert of the Machynlleth Festival, Julie Watts of the Tenby Festival, Geraint Lewis of the North Wales (St Asaph) and John S Davies of the Fishguard Festivals, Roy Bohana when at the Welsh Arts Council, David Russell Hulme of Aberystwyth Philomusica, and Keith Smith of Southampton YO; also I have cherished the friendship of

Andrew Neill and many members of the Elgar Society, similarly of Patrick Mills, founder of the Peter Warlock Society; also of George Davies, whose camera work adorned my book on Peter Warlock, and Dr Lyn Davies, who helped to put me 'On the Road with Elinor' on TV in 1993; and of the many enthusiastic workers in the Guild for the Promotion of Welsh Music and in the Incorporated Society of Musicians.

But particularly in recent years I have been inspired not only by John Turner, who got me to treat the recorder as a serious musical instrument, but more especially by my second wife, Jeanne.

Ian with Jeanne, Christmas 1995

Notes to Part Three

[1] Dr David Harries died on December 25th 2002 at the age of sixty-nine.
[2] See my *The Crying Curlew: Peter Warlock* [Gomer, Llandysul, Ceredigion, 1994; Wm Elkin, Nov 2001]
[3] *Heresies of Our Time* by Ian Parrott (*The Modern Churchman*, 1981)
[4] M Maeterlinck: *The Supreme Law* [Rider & Co.]
[5] Dorothy L Sayers: *The Mind of the Maker* [Methuen, 1941]

Appendix 1

Articles

(a) *Influences on My Music*
by
Ian Parrott

Extract from *Musical Opinion*, April 1983

1 EGYPT

After volunteering to fight the Germans, many of us at the beginning of the Second World War found ourselves on the High Seas travelling to a very distant land and a very unpredictable future. Being crammed into a converted luxury liner bound for somewhere round the Cape was probably not unlike the three-week voyage to the Falklands — though we did have the German warships *Scharnhorst*, *Gneisenau* and *Prinz Eugen* in the Atlantic at the same time.

I mention this not just because of the happier moments when changing ships in South Africa, which meant conducting the Durban Orchestra and also hearing the broadcast of a song which I had written at sea. The bigger stimulus was to come later: the Western Desert. Awe-inspiring at the best of times, it became even more momentous for us young soldiers who, at that stage, lived with no encouraging news — the only outlook then was that the Germans were well on the way to winning.

The song already written, a setting of Lermontov (in Russian), was later joined by others to form *Four Songs of Absence*: a setting of Kerner's German text *Wie dir, so mir* in 1942 and of John Donne's *Absence* in January the following year, when the Eighth Army had advanced a thousand miles over the desert — the fortunes of war had indeed changed since El Alamein, about which I also wrote in a symphonic impression. The fourth song, 1944, was a setting of Beddoes' *How many times do I love thee*.

Other works to be inspired by the strange dry, hot fly-blown world of North Africa included two movements for string quartet — one was actually broadcast on Cairo Radio — based on ideas that came to me during the quieter moments in the desert. An enjoyable contrast was a burlesque opera, *The Sergeant-Major's Daughter*, performed in various services establishments and finally in 'Music for All' in Cairo in July 1943. Coping with such crises as having the leading tenor posted to India a few days before a performance was one of the hazards. At one time when I was up the desert, I communicated with my librettist via a priority air bag.

What might be called 'popular music' of all sorts, hymns, camp fire tunes, Beatles, etc., has never stuck with me. I cannot even remember any of it; I cannot rub two notes together on the tune, let alone harmonise anything for a sing-song. If, exceptionally, certain Lutheran chorales do stick, it is because of Bach and my effort to remember the sequence of notes. (I cannot stand Victorian hymns.) Or there may be an 'association' thing. On radio, during the advance of the Eighth Army, I remember, exceptionally, a tune of the day, *I can't give you anything but love, baby*. It did make an impression and, after making the intellectual effort to memorise it, I used a parody of it in the opera. At least the 'light' music of that period was infinitely better than the thump 'musak' which, inexplicably, is considered today to be an essential and constant background to civilized living. [1] If music is worth listening to, it should be in the foreground.

My Theme and Six Variants for piano, also dating from those years, was published and played widely, reaching Town Hall, New York, with Eunice Eaton as soloist in April 1950.

The most important composition to be directly inspired, however, was the symphonic impression, *Luxor*. Very shortly before the battle of El Alamein, I was sent on leave to Upper Egypt. Fascinated by the tombs of the kings on the 'dead' (West) side of the Nile, I was even more impressed by the vast ancient buildings on the 'side of life' (the East). Ancient Egypt recognised that life depended utterly on the regular movement of the sun from East to West and also on the constant flowing of the river from South to North. After looking at the temple of Luxor, I discovered that there were signs of younger civilizations excavated and tucked into corners of the vast structure: a Roman temple, a Christian altar and — the baby at only 800 years old — a Moslem mosque. The mosque, incidentally, is much higher up than the others because of the accumulation of sand over the centuries.

A rondo with the main Egyptian theme to dominate came to me immediately. Though I would have thought that Holst might have been behind my style, my friend, Dr Frederic Wood, later suggested that, with its Lydian line, it could well have come to me in an extrasensory way direct from ancient Egypt. The other characterisations, Roman, Christian and Moslem, were able to come to the fore, but the Egyptian main subject was never far away. This composition was awarded the First Prize of the Royal Philharmonic Society in November 1949 and played by the LPO under Boult the following year

2 WALES

When I arrived to take up the professorship at Aberystwyth in 1950, Welsh music was still decidedly 'provincial', showing little sign of continental influence in harmony, rhythm or orchestration. It is possible that the idea of large many-note chords, such as I used to represent three vast obelisks in *Luxor*, got into the music of the young and, as yet not well-known, Alun Hoddinott.

Be that as it may (*Luxor* was given by the LSO at the National Eisteddfod of 1952), there is no doubt that I soon found myself deeply involved in a musical revolution spearheaded by a man of vision called John Edwards. I have written elsewhere [2] of this farsighted idealist and of the Guild for the Promotion of Welsh Music, which he founded and of which I was proud to be a foundation member.

There are still signs of conservatism in the more worried nationalist corners of Welsh life, but most thinking musicians have willingly enlarged and expanded their modes of expression.

Writing the incidental music for the BBC feature, *Prince Hywel's Last Poem* by Sir Idris Bell, made me delve into Welsh history; and the titles of three piano pieces of 1951 I took from the Robert ap Huw MS: Gosteg, Profiad and Caniad.

The biggest effect of the Welsh environment, however, came when I completed the opera, *The Black Ram*, to a bilingual text: English libretto by Sir Idris Bell and Welsh words by Sir Thomas Parry-Williams. Although we had given our own College performance of the Overture and Prologue in 1952, the work as a whole was not finished until the next year. A version of the overture for large orchestra was first performed by the Hallé under Barbirolli in Newtown. Various extracts were given from time to time and a concert version to the Welsh text was broadcast from the Welsh region of the BBC, conducted by Arwel Hughes, early in 1957 and repeated on 'Overseas'. In spite of Hans Redlich's persuasive article, 'A New Welsh Folk Opera', in *Music & Letters* (April 1956), and with other signs of support, including Bernard Rands in *Yr Arloeswr* (January 1958), the opera had to wait until March 1966 before it reached the stage.

Then it was performed by amateurs and received with great enthusiasm at the Kings Hall, Aberystwyth, but was not taken up professionally. On a lurid tale, basically true, of a bad baronet in the 18th century, the work made extensive use of Welsh folk-tunes, a dance, *Abergenny*, and a fine old hymn, *Braint*.

In 1954, I arranged three old Welsh airs for two recorders and harp: *Dygan Caersws, Hoffedd Hywel ab Owain Gwynedd* and *Dadl Dau*. Sir Idris Bell supplied me with his version of a *Child's Hunting Song* from the 7th century Gododdin and also Huw Morus' *Carol Plygain*, which I set in theWelsh.

It was a natural challenge to write for the harp, the most Welsh of instruments, which I did several times. *Ceredigion* of 1957, receiving its first performance by Ann Griffiths in Israel, was taken up by Osian Ellis and had performances ranging from Moscow (Vera Dulova) to the USA (Phyllis Schlomovitz recorded it in 1970).

Elinor Bennett gave first performance of *Arfon* at the North Wales Festival of 1978.

1958 saw the completion of three folk-song settings for orchestra for the BBC's *Aelwyd y Gân* with Emrys Cleaver. These were *Hen Ferchetan, Mae Nghariad i'n Fenws* and *Cwyn Mam y'Nghyfraith* — *Three Ladies*, with very different characters.

In 1959 I managed O level Welsh — with 'oral proficiency', though I have lapsed sadly since then.

The overture, *Seithenin*, was first performed by the BBC Welsh Orchestra in 1959 and it was included in a tour of Wales by the LPO under Wyn Morris and Sir Adrian Boult in 1964. I cannot be sure whether the inspiration was entirely Welsh in such works as the Cor Anglais Concerto (Roger Winfield and Hallé with Barbirolli, Cheltenham Festival., July 1958) or the Cello Concerto (Pleeth, 1961) or in the first of four string quartets and the opera, *Once Upon a Time*, based on a Russian short story. Perhaps Leighton Thomas was right when he described me as "A Many-sided Composer" in the *Western Mail* of November 18 1961.[3] The Septet (1962) was first given at the Cheltenham Festival of that year by the Virtuoso Ensemble and the following year I wrote a *Jubilate Deo* which was first performed at the Arts Council, London, in 1967.

Organ music was there too. The Toccata was written and first performed in 1962 (Peter Boorman, St. John's College, Cambridge); *Mosaics* (1968) was first given in 1969 (Rodney Baldwyn, Pershore Abbey) and Fantasia (1974) was broadcast by Royston Havard. The later Suite (1977) was first performed in its entirety by Andrew Sidebottom in Westminster Abbey, though the last movement ('Homage to Two Masters') was played by Jennifer Bate and Gillian Weir.

Lest it be thought that the Welsh influence was diluted, I must say that there were works also like the brass band *Land of Song* — a test piece in 1970 — and *The Song of the Stones of St Davids*, which appeared on a gramophone record in 1969. And one of my most recent works is the chamber opera, *Blodeuedd* (*The Lady of Flowers*), on a subject from the Mabinogion (1981).

3 NEW ZEALAND

New Zealand is as far away as you can go without taking off for the moon. Even so, thanks to the overseas examining tours which I made for Trinity College of Music, London, I have visited the country twice.

I was already moved to write a second symphony when I set off on the first of these tours in 1960. Although the first ideas, later to be used in the second movement, came to me in Norfolk, Virginia, the main themes were composed when I had lost a day crossing the date-line and had spent some time avoiding falling coconuts in a jungle hut in Fiji. New Zealand had great natural beauty from the fascinating mudpools of the North Island to the grandeur of the Southern Alps. I was also attracted to the Maori words and to the sounds of the native birds, especially to the bell bird, more than the tui, whose clear single notes we listened to along the shores of Lake Rotuiti, south of Nelson, in particular.

The score of Symphony No.2 was completed back at home in Aberystwyth in 1961. Its sub-title was 'Round the World'.

In 1970 I was on a second world tour, this time accompanied by Mrs. Parrott. Although we took in the Southern States instead of Canada, I had another spell of examining in exotic Fiji — this time we had a puncture but enjoyed using a hired car to get across the island. One of the main artistic results on this occasion was Wind Quintet No.2.[†] Written mostly in Palmerston North — in the evenings after each long day's examining — I was concerned to portray 'Windy Wellington' and rough weather generally. The sub-title of this composition, which had been commissioned by the BBC Cardiff, was 'Fresh about Cook Strait', which is in fact a local weather forecast expression. The work was played again, soon after our return, in the Bromsgrove Festival.

---

† Now published by Phylloscopus

Fresh about Cook Strait: the opening bars of the Wind Quintet No.2

Although I wrote other works at the time and also finished reading the proofs of the Master Musicians *Elgar* [4] while in New Zealand, I never wrote with more enthusiasm than in the wind quintet which, while being mainly blustery, had a peaceful aleatoric section called 'Bell birds in the bush', in which I exploited various effects on flute, oboe, clarinet, bassoon and horn.

At one time at Trinity College I had given harmony lessons to the great Maori singer, Inia Te Wiata. Although he showed a certain reluctance to tackle the niceties of music theory, he became a very fine bass singer. In June 1970, which was twenty years later, we had the pleasure of having a short chat with him, when he appeared in a concert in Wellington with the Aotearoa Maori Group and the National Band of New Zealand.

There has always been enthusiasm for other composers, [5] great masters of the past and also living composers, especially at this time for those living in the Commonwealth — whose music I introduced later to the audiences of Wales.

In 1974 I contributed a variation on a theme of Vernon Griffiths to a set of variations in honour of the 80th birthday of my old friend, the retired professor of music at the University of Canterbury at Christchurch. Not only had Vernon Griffiths modelled his department to some extent on that at Aberystwyth, particularly with regard to the employment of executants, but he had also done me the honour on my previous visit in 1960 of putting on a concert of my works.

If my second symphony had been outward looking across the world, the next was to be introspective. Indeed, the slow movement of Symphony No.3 (1966) involved contemplating a single chord in Tchaikovsky. Another unusual feature was the use of an obbligato string quartet throughout.

Perhaps this serious work may lead to the next section on the less obvious influences that have affected my music.

I have also been interested in the technicalities of music theory, [6] which will sometimes be discernible in my compositions perhaps, as in Elgar, by my going against rather than with any regulations.

4 PSYCHICAL RESEARCH

In addition to the stimulus which has come from various parts of the physical world I have long been motivated by my awareness of the 'other world'. Words such as paranormal and extrasensory and 'creationist' had not been coined when I first thought of the non-physical more than forty years ago. But now I can write a Foreword to a book called *Life Unlimited* [7] in which I show puzzlement that the 'Third World' (the majority of mankind) can happily believe in the reality of an unseen world, while modern Western civilization, no less than the Eastern bloc, looks down on its belief as primitive and ignorant.

Perhaps it is not too surprising that the finale to my Symphony No.1, completed in 1945, was based on an earlier piece of 1941 called *A Dream*, some of which was actually composed in a dream.

When I was in the Western Desert, a friend of mine went to his CO to ask for 'compassionate leave', because his mother was dangerously ill. Some days later he had a 'noninferential awareness' that she had died. So strong was this awareness that he asked the CO to cancel the leave. With the Germans in control of the Mediterranean, mail from home would take as much as nine weeks. Nine weeks later a letter arrived confirming the exact time of death.

Though believing that the above was an example of extrasensory perception, I hasten to say that I am not entirely gullible. When I was sleeping in a hole in the sand one night when we were being bombed, I was surprised to find that I woke up on three occasions just *before* the explosion. It may appear unexpected, but the correct explanation is that the sound waves reached me through the sand in time for me to wake up and hear the *same* sound waves through the air.

Believing that all genuine composers have access to a world 'beyond' this one, I would naturally be drawn to a poet such as Flecker, in whose *In Phaeacia* [8] are lines such as 'our garden that goes on for ever Out of the world'. Down-to-earthers often accept poetry when they would reject the same ideas in prose. In 1948 I contributed a short article on 'Inspiration' to *The Chesterian* and the next year I gave one of my talks on 'The Mind of the Creative Artist' at Birmingham University Extra-Mural Department. In 1957, an article appeared in *The Birmingham Post* on 'Psychical Research: Experiences of a Composer' and another in *The Listener* on 'The Significance of Parapsychology'. I even crossed swords with the formidable Professor Antony Flew. I wrote on 'The Group Mind' in *Light* (Winter 1959) and on 'Synchronicity in Dreams' in the Journal of the Society for Psychical Research (June 1961). These were followed by many more such articles up to 'The Case for the Spiritual View Today' (*The Modern Churchman* 1980), etc.

It looks almost as if I wrote as many words as notes. The words did rub off, I think. After I had completed a book in 1962 on the music which the younger of the two ladies, Miss Jourdain, heard at Versailles in 1902, [9] I made a reconstruction of the sort of music which I think she might have heard — something like Philidor, Monsigny and Grétry.

In 1967 I wrote a piece called *Pant Glas* — an idyll for violin, glockenspiel and piano. The glockenspiel was a direct reference to the goats with bells at the 'Valley of Animals', where Elma Williams wrote her best-seller of that name. Although pronounced incurably ill, Miss Williams kept herself alive by her belief and stamina to write more inspired novels. In the same year I met Rosemary Brown for the first time at Attingham Park, an Adult College in Shropshire. A few years later, for the retirement celebrations of its enlightened warden, Sir George Trevelyan, I wrote *Reaching for the Light* for small orchestra, piano and harpsichord. It was meant faithfully to portray Sir George's philosophy in musical language.

Rosemary Brown became a close personal friend and my wife did a portrait of her which was used as frontispiece to my book. [10] While Rosemary was 'sitting', Mrs. Parrott started to think of Chopin and of Delacroix's portrait. Rosemary suddenly said in her quiet matter-of-fact voice, "Oh, I'm sorry, I nearly said that in Chopin's accent. He's standing by me". Apart from helping Basil Ramsey and others to prepare the best of her remarkable compositions for publication [11], I took part in an exciting occasion in 1976, a Dutch television film on her. It involved being seen and heard and also orchestrating a movement which she had 'received' from Beethoven. I sometimes say with a wry smile that if I write a new piece of my own it is not immediately taken up, but if I orchestrate a piece of Rosemary Brown in August it is performed by the Radio Philharmonic Orchestra under a leading Dutch conductor, David Porcelijn, in September — to more than four million viewers!

My Three Thoughtful Songs of 1977 (broadcast by Kenneth Bowen in 1982) were settings of Blake, Jane Wilson and Gerard Manley Hopkins, with views on mortality from the 18th, 20th and 19th centuries.

In case it be thought that I am making myself out to be some sort of a saint, I should mention that the stimulus for the Sinfonietta of 1978 — number four in my symphonies — came from a competition — which I did not win. Anway, Symphony No.5, an extrovert, happy composition of 1979, has been enjoyed wherever it has been given.

No one but a fool would fail to derive satisfaction from a no-nonsense commission or from the challenge of actual instruments — my Concertino for Two Guitars (1973) is an example of the latter.

It is quite a time since the BBC put on my Fantasy and Allegro for two pianos, representative of a 'Contemporary British Composer' in 1947. I have not ceased to be a writer just because I am older; and I have kept in touch with my old friend Humphrey Searle (who died in May last year) despite our entirely different views on compositional technique. One thing he shared with me was an interest in the journals, *Psychic News* and *Two Worlds* when edited by the warm-hearted Maurice Barbanell. His newsagent used to say, "Here's yer 'Cycling News' and yer 'Two Wheels' ".

Notes

[1] This bugbear I have dealt with more than once in letters to newspapers and journals and especially in *Music Teacher*. 'Compulsory Music', 1961, and 'More Compulsory Music', 1967.

[2] *The Story of the Guild for the Promotion of Welsh Music 1955-1980*. A symposium edited by Ian Parrott [Angel Chambers, 94 Walter Road, Swansea SA1 5QA]

[3] Leighton Thomas also wrote 'Ian Parrott at Fifty' for *The Musical Times*, March 1966.

[4] *Elgar* by Ian Parrott [Dent, 1971, Second Impression 1977]

[5] I have written on some of these already. See my 'Another Personal Credo', *Musical Opinion*, October 1975.

[6] For example: 'Imaginary Roots', *Music Teacher*, January 1951; 'Changed Notes', *Musical Times*, June 1955; 'Fugue without Tears', *Music Teacher*, 1970

[7] *Life Unlimited* by Allan Barham [Volturna Press, 1982]

[8] My setting was published by Lengnick in 1945.

[9] *The Music of 'An Adventure'* by Ian Parrott [Regency, 1966]

[10] *The Music of Rosemary Brown* by Ian Parrott [Regency, 1978]

[11] For example, *Music from Beyond* [B Ramsey, 1976]

(b) *Globetrotting*
by
Ian Parrott

Extract from *The Western Mail*, January 14 1961

Early in 1960 I left Britain to undertake an overseas examining tour for the Trinity College of Music, London, which took me right round the world. Apart from the practical examinations which were most interesting and varied, I had the experience of visiting university establishments in the New World and in Australasia, acting as external assessor to the music department of the University of Canterbury, New Zealand.

The tour was marked at both ends by concerts which I shall not easily forget; on May 11 some leading Philadelphia artists performed 'Contemporary Welsh Composers' at Rutgers University, Camden, USA, and I was invited to be the guest speaker by the organiser, Dr Claire Polin, one of whose works I had arranged to have played at Aberystwyth in February. As a result we had launched a series of 'exchange' concerts between the United States and the rest of the world.

Then at the very end of my tour I was honoured by a concert of my own compositions excellently played by the finest New Zealand artists in Christchurch on December 3. This concert was made possible by the enthusiasm and energy of the professor of music of Canterbury University, Vernon Griffiths. I felt once again what I had felt in the States, the generosity and kindness of local people the world over.

Memorable
The first part of the tour started in New York where I met William Schuman, president of the Juilliard School, and five other Eastern States with a visit to Washington, DC. Then I crossed the border in a bus to Montreal and was fascinated by the change, the Canadian way of life and the French influence. Ontario was a memorable province for me for many things musical. In London (Ontario) — which I went to via Paris (Ontario)! — I heard two magnificent organists who played the Hindemith Sonata No.1.

In Toronto I visited the Conservatorium and saw the room where students listen to stereophonic records with earphones, one channel on the right and one on the left, while they follow the scores. I met the Dean, Boyd Neel, and had a very pleasant dinner with him, and also met two of the leading Canadian composers, John Beckwith and John Cook — the latter was writing music for a Shakespeare Festival at Stratford (again Ontario).

Organists
Geoffrey Payzant, philosopher and writer on music, was also an interesting personality with whom I exchanged ideas on music and telepathy; and Ezra Schabas, clarinettist, told me of how he had played Alun Hoddinott's Clarinet Concerto in Toronto with great success and pleasure. I addressed the Royal Canadian College of Organists and met Dr Healey Willan, the distinguished organist.

In Winnipeg I met Capt. Armand Ferland, French-speaking Canadian band-master, who had a score of Bliss's Clarinet Quintet inscribed to him. Before his military band played the Brahms *Academic Festival Overture* to me, the sergeant got them all to their feet with a "Band!—'Shun!".

Then across the prairies to Calgary and the Rockies. In 1875, when the College at Aberystwyth was starting, Calgary consisted of two tents surrounded by Red Indians. Now it has the finest auditorium that I've ever seen in the world, far better than the Festival Hall. In Aberystwyth, we still haven't a concert hall worthy of a University town. The Old World moves more slowly than the New.

After a trip in Canadian Pacific Airlines through Honolulu and Fiji, I arrived to a second winter and ten degrees of frost at Dunedin in the South Island of New Zealand. After a couple of weeks examining there, I moved to Christchurch. Professor Vernon Griffiths, Professor of Music at Canterbury University, Christchurch, who met me at the airport with the Press, had modelled his department to a great extent on the pattern of the University of Wales, especially Aberystwyth College, which he visited in 1952. In particular, he was proud of his string trio and piano quartet.

He has recently acquired a harpsichord as well. In a way, he has beaten us to it, as his 'Violin leader' is a BA of Cambridge and can lecture to the students as well as perform chamber music, while his cellist is an expert on acoustics. Also amongst his talented staff is the composer, John Ritchie.

My examining was confined to the South Island where there was plenty of talent, imagination and hard work, but I managed to get in a visit to the North Island for a short holiday in September. This included seeing the vast kauri trees, the glow-worm caves of Waitomo and the thermal region of Rotorua. But the most majestic and magnificent scenery was to be found in the south, where Mount Cook, "the Cloud Piercer", rises to 12,349 ft, higher than any peak in the whole of Australasia; also Milford Sound, with Mitre Peak rising sheer from sea level to 5,560 ft.

Concert
It was scenes like these that consolidated the musical thoughts which I had jotted down some time back in the States and Canada. As I travelled round New Zealand, so the themes and motives became larger sections of a symphony. One movement was completed and another was nearly finished in full score by the time I returned home.

I couldn't call this work ' From the New World', as Dvorák had immortalised that title, but I might call it 'Round the World'!

I have the happiest memories of the University people in Dunedin, the kindness of the Vice-Chancellor and many members of the staff. In Invercargill I actually met two Prime Ministers; one was Leader of the Opposition at the time, but they had a General Election on November 26! Then there was the magnificent send-off in Christchurch on December 3, the concert of my compositions by such splendid performers as Maurice Till and Michael Toovey, pianists, and this included the first performance of the comic opera *Once upon a Time* (libretto by Cecil Price of UCW, Aberystwyth), which went down extremely well with the audience.

A few days in Sydney completed a most stimulating and exciting tour, in which I had examined over 3,500 candidates, some of a very high standard, before I flew home through Singapore and India, thus completing the circuit of the globe.

(c) *Thirty-three Years in Welsh Music* *
by
Ian Parrott

Extract from *Welsh Music*, Spring 1983, Vol.7, No.3

When I first came to the Music Department at UCW Aberystwyth in 1950, I found I had two lecturers to work with me: Charles Clements and John Clapham. Both of them rehearsed and played in the weekly chamber music concerts — piano and cello — for which they received not a single extra penny. A very different situation exists today, where live adequately paid executant/teachers undertake this practical work and where a senior lecturer, two lecturers, a tutor through the medium of Welsh and a University Fellow undertake the scholarly work. The number of full-time music students in 1950 was less than twenty. By 1980 we had topped the ninety mark, including postgraduates.

Principal Ifor L Evans, a somewhat fiery character, was interested in many things — not always advantageous to those who specialised in them. These included theology and music, so one's heart sank when it became obvious that his own hymns were of more interest than anything new. The chamber music players were sometimes summoned to play at Plas Penglais as if they were employed by an eighteenth century Viennese nobleman.

Once, when Edward Bor (the leader) noticed that the Principal had not arrived for a concert, so they would wait — this was just before my time — the wife of the zoology professor shouted: "Damn the Principal, I'm here". The second violin at that time had previously been a student. I arranged to employ Logan Lewis, a member of a distinguished Welsh musical family. He played violin for the College in the daytime for the handsome sum of £50 a session and played trumpet in a dance band in the evenings. When I suggested to the College Treasurer that he might be paid more for his playing, the answer came: "Could he not do some *work*?" Unmusical though solicitor Ivor Evans (not to be confused with Ifor L) might have been, his wife, Mrs Elsie Evans, was a particularly good and sensitive pianist. She played two-piano music with me and with

---

* Professor Parrott retires this year [1983] from the Gregynog Chair of Music at Aberystwyth.

Dorothy Wilson, piano teacher from Borth, and she was a good sight-reader. We had many happy soirées at her house, Carreg Wen.

Another place for soirées was Bron Castell, Capel Bangor, the home of Jack and Peggy Challinor, and here the music room, over a stable, was approached from the house across a romantic footbridge.

The Laugharne-born viola player, Raymond Jeremy, was a considerable asset until his retirement in 1958. Having made records with the Virtuoso Quartet and other ensembles, he had been involved in the first performances of some of Elgar's and Vaughan Williams's later compositions; and his great technique and musicianship were matched by a warm and friendly personality. Once, he told me, he was playing *Gerontius* under Elgar's baton. As a viola player he was almost literally under the great composer's nose. In the middle of the performance, Elgar leant over to him and whispered: "I still like this, you know".

By the end of the first session the College Orchestra and Choir had played music by Walford Davies and David de Lloyd, my predecessors, and the Franck Symphonic Variations, with Charles Clements as outstanding pianist. The following year our December concert included one of my first students, Kenneth Bowen — described then as a baritone.

At a very early stage I set about reviving the Music Club. Principal Ifor L Evans had not encouraged Town and Gown to get together, but by May 1951 I was able to persuade the retired French lecturer Dr A B Thomas to act as treasurer. He was the horn player with a deformed right hand who had been 'discovered' by Walford Davies in the twenties. The first secretary was Dr E G Healey of Zoology and we ran the whole thing unaided from the Music House, using the Examination Hall for concerts. Sir Bryner Jones was our first president.

Another link, broken during the de Lloyd period (1927-1948), was that with Gregynog. When I renewed it, Dr Thomas Jones, then President of the College, was particularly pleased and expressed the wish that it should be maintained. (He then lived in Aberystwyth until his death in 1955.) As a result I was able to run a series of post-war festivals (1955 to 1961) for Miss Margaret Davies at the mansion. If not so lavish as those of the twenties and thirties organised for her more dominating sister Gwendoline, at least we had some very good music making, to which I was able to invite such distinguished composers as Bliss and Rubbra.

As said above, one of my first students to achieve fame was Kenneth Bowen. (He made a graceful reference to these early days in a programme on Radio Wales on November 7 1982.) We gave our first First Class Honours BA in my time, in June 1951, to Arthur Hefin Jones (I was pleased to see him conducting on BBC1 *Songs of Praise* on October 30 1982); and the following year to Jayne Filer (whose daughter has followed in her footsteps).

When I had written the incidental music for Sir Idris Bell's BBC feature *Prince Hywel's Last Poem* (July 1952), we got down to the serious business of writing an opera, *The Black Ram*. Sir Thomas Parry-Williams (knighted 1958) had already willingly done such jobs for me as translating Mussorgsky's *Gopak* from Russian into Welsh for student Gaynor Evans (now Mrs Hall) to sing. He now joined us so that a simultaneous Welsh text could be available for the new opera.

In August 1952, my symphonic poem, *Luxor*, was featured by the LSO at the National Eisteddfod in Aberystwyth — soon afterwards my other 'Egyptian' period piece, *El Alamein*, was broadcast by the BBC Scottish.

After the war, when most musical rats were racing towards the big city, I was moving away from London, via Birmingham, to Wales. It may have meant losing the glue-pot contacts which make friends and influence publishers, but richer intangible rewards came from a new rural world of West Wales with its folk-heritage — certainly my compositions flourished, and I was busy writing for the German *Musik in Geschichte und Gegenwart*. Its British representative, Hans Redlich, I was to invite over to conduct his edition of Monteverdi's *Vespers* in Llanbadarn Church in March 1955. He described the acoustics as up to St Mark's, Venice.

Ian and Elizabeth with Yehudi Menuhin at Worcester, c1970

Once Upon a Time : the Aberystwyth performers, November 1961
Back row, left to right: Dr Ron Walker, Ian, Charles Clements, Prof Cecil Price
Front row: Kenneth Bowen, Eirioes Thomas, Redvers Llewellyn

One of the hazards of translating for a foreign encyclopaedia, I remember, was when I was writing an article on Daniel Jones. I intended to say that this Welsh composer "was *not* consciously influenced" by folk music. It nearly appeared in the German equivalent as "was *un*consciously influenced"!

After a visit from Cardiff College of Music and Drama students (directed by Alun Hoddinott), another young student featured in our own 1953 December concert. This was William Mathias, who brilliantly played the piano part in Lambert's *Rio Grande*. In 1954 he joined the company of First Classes.

The overture to the as yet unfinished opera, *The Black Ram*, was performed by the Hallé Orchestra under Sir John Barbirolli at the Montgomery County Music Festival in May 1954. This was also the time of the founding of the Guild for the Promotion of Welsh Music under the inspiring leadership of John Edwards, about which I have written elsewhere. [1] "Welsh Music? I didn't know there was any", said a professor at the RAM in 1930. [2]

The College orchestra had the honour of playing before Her Majesty the Queen, when she opened the completed building of the National Library of Wales on August 8 1955.

The Black Ram, a direct result of a feeling of personal involvement in Cardiganshire, was taken up by Opera da Camera, who performed extracts in Birmingham in May 1956; and the overture was broadcast by the BBC Welsh Orchestra under Mansel Thomas in November of that same year. Undoubtedly, however, the broadcast of a concert version to the Welsh text in February 1957 was a high spot in the opera's life. The conductor was Arwel Hughes, and many distinguished singers took the solo parts. In spite of much enthusiasm and advocacy in many quarters and a further broadcast on the Overseas Service of the BBC, the work was still not taken up in its entirety by any professional company.

In 1959 one of my pleasures was making folk-song arrangements for the BBC's *Aelwyd y Gân* with Emrys Cleaver. After the tunes which had been integrated into the opera, I found three more — later made into a Suite, *The Three Ladies*. Another pleasure of that year was acting as pilot for the 'grand whirlwind tour' of Wales undertaken by Sir Arthur Bliss, Master of the Queen's Music, starting with a Guild dinner in Cardiff, staying with the Trahernes; a visit to John Edwards's record factory in Pontardawe, a concert in Aberystwyth in which two students appeared — William Mathias with his Opus 1 and Roy Bohana as madrigal conductor — and a final visit to Gregynog to hear the choir.

Life for me in Aberystwyth was interrupted twice when I accepted invitations to undertake overseas examining tours for the Trinity College of Music, London. In 1960 the way to Fiji and New Zealand was via Canada; in 1970 it was by way of the Bahamas and the Southern States of the USA. I was able to maintain and make valuable University links, none more important than that with the University of Canterbury at Christchurch, New Zealand, where Professor Vernon Griffiths (already using executants in the Aberystwyth way) was such a live wire — followed by Professor John Ritchie, later to be General Secretary of the International Society for Music Education.

In the early years, when Carpenter Hall was a hostel for women students, an attractive feature organised by the Warden, Mrs Gwladys Morgan Jones, was an annual carol concert. On their return from holidays abroad, many of the girls brought back unusual and exotic carols to be added to the collection.

In 1963 Charles Clements, senior lecturer in the Music Department and organist at Seilo, much loved and respected by all, retired and was given a Presentation Dinner in the manner of a *This is your Life*. Contributors to the prize fund included Sir Adrian Boult, Elsie Suddaby, Jelly d'Arányi and the Lady Davies of Llandinam. He had completed 43 years in the Music Department and was shortly to play in the thousandth weekly concert of the series. Redvers Llewellyn, himself a great artist, was one of his colleagues who paid tribute and Mrs Parrott presented a cheque and pencil box. The organisation was in the hands of David Harries (then lecturer), who next year was also the able manager of a big tenth annual congress of the Guild for the Promotion of Welsh Music held in Aberystwyth, featuring many Welsh composers and performers as well as Sir Michael Tippett. 1964 was the year in which I found myself External Examiner in three universities: Bristol, Manchester and Leicester; and also gave the Gresham Lectures in music in London.

At last *The Black Ram* found the stage, albeit the stage of the King's Hall, Aberystwyth, where there was no pit for the orchestra, and where the chorus had to rush across the road at the back to change costumes — it was March 1966. Great enthusiasm was engendered and large audiences came for the three nights. For this fiftieth birthday year a Wigmore Hall recital, the Harriet Cohen Musicology Medal and a *Songs of Praise* conducting on the BBC appeared shortly afterwards.

The Times of April 25 1967 reminded its readers that the idea of resident chamber ensembles in university music departments was then close on half a century old. It was gratifying to read that *"pride of place properly belongs to Aberystwyth, where Sir Walford Davies appointed professional chamber musicians as long ago as 1919; an idea which was soon taken up at Bangor and Cardiff and which probably first brought about a realisation of the benefits to be had ... benefits now appreciated as far afield as California and Canterbury, New Zealand."*

This, I seem to remember, was about the time that I passed O level Welsh with 'oral proficiency' — though I fear that I never kept it up as I should — sitting with the children, and not presiding, was salutary.

It was thanks to my old friend, A T Shaw of Worcester, virtual founder and 'father' of the now flourishing Elgar Society, of which I am a Vice-President, that in 1968 I gave the first of many talks on the *Enigma* in Malvern. This led eventually to my being asked by Sir Jack Westrup to write the Master Musicians *Elgar*, and it was in Carmarthen that Bishop John Richards put me on the right lines for solving the Enigma's 'dark saying'. In March 1977, Mrs Parrott presented her painting of Elgar's house, Plas Gwyn, to Sir Adrian Boult just before his ninetieth birthday.

1968 saw the arrival of Americans from Yale University in Wrexham to honour Elihu Yale, who gave his name to the University 250 years ago. My concerto for trombone and wind band was brilliantly played on this occasion (soloist R de Prospo). Mr Kingman Brewster, president of Yale (later American Ambassador), laid a wreath on Elihu Yale's tomb.

After some delay, my book on those great patrons of the arts, the sisters

Gwendoline and Margaret Davies of Gregynog, *The Spiritual Pilgrims*, appeared.

We had the honour of HRH Prince Charles with us as a very conscientious student in 1969. After he had attended a Music Department concert (and had actually read my new book) I introduced some of the staff. Hoping to say something useful I mentioned that Dr Owain Edwards spoke Welsh and his wife spoke Norwegian. Looking them up and down, the Prince asked: "And how do you converse?" Shortly afterwards Mrs Parrott and I were commanded to attend the Investiture at Caernarfon. With us were Mr and Mrs Hamilton Lokey from Atlanta, Georgia. Since Mr Lokey had been a generous benefactor of the church at Llanbadarn, Bishop Richards had arranged the visit. In fact, Mr Lokey had walked down the aisle with the vicar, who said that the roof needed repairing. "How much would it cost?", he asked. The vicar (Canon Walter Emlyn Davies), thinking it to be an academic question, mentioned a sum running into several hundreds of pounds — and Mr Lokey wrote out a cheque there and then! So the vicar told the bishop, and the bishop told the palace ...

It was about this time that I was visiting Attingham Park (the Adult College near Shrewsbury) at the invitation of the warden, Sir George Trevelyan. There I met Rosemary Brown for the first time and developed not only an enthusiasm for the music which came through her but also a friendship with a sincere and modest person. For Sir George's Retirement Party in August 1971, I wrote some music, *Reaching for the Light*. There was also much celebrating, including the ascent of a hot air balloon. In November that year I played some of Rosemary Brown's music at a concert at the College in memory of Elma Williams, author of the best selling novel about nearby Pant Glas, *The Valley of Animals*.

At a time when Bangor College could say that there had been a couple of Principals since its foundation, we at Aberystwyth were going through a stormy period. Ifor L Evans died in 1952 and was followed by an acting principal, Professor Lily Newton, until the appointment of the controversial Goronwy Rees, who was soon asked to resign. Another interim period with Professor Morton was followed by Thomas Parry. There were now therefore no more Armistice Services. No longer did we use Ifor L Evans's Service Book; and no more did I have to waken an executant from a semi-reverent somnolence to give us a note in order to sing David de Lloyd's three-fold *Amen*. So times changed.

The Christian Aid concerts, however, became the annual responsibility of Mrs Parrott and myself. At that time I used to play piano duets with Charles Clements. In 1971 'Charlie', as he was affectionately known, also conducted the Aberystwyth Singers, a group with whom he had been associated for forty years or so.

There were, sadly, not many lucid years in his company. At one time he had a formidable reputation as a pianist, organist and, particularly accompanist. In 1922 he had 'turned over' for Bartók, when that as yet not very well-known composer paid a fleeting visit to Aberystwyth. He also overheard Walford Davies, in spite of a confident outward manner, whisper, "Baffling, isn't it?", when Bartók's percussive playing of *Allegro Barbaro*, etc., was over. Now Charlie's memory was starting to deteriorate (this was as early as 1973) and by the summer of 1976 at the age of 78 he was admitted to St David's Hospital, Carmarthen.

David Harries shared with me the pleasure of representing Welsh Music in Dublin in June 1971 for a 'Wythnos Cerdd' — a useful contact.

Radio 3 ran a series of talks in early 1972 called *The Faculty of Music* in which several professors of music took part. Being sandwiched between Denny of Leeds and Keys of Birmingham, I tried to predict 'The Direction of University Music' — but I don't think we foresaw the hard times of the present cuts.

Bishop B N Y Vaughan felt that some of the rhythmic joy of the Latin American peoples could get into our Welsh services. Although Welsh folk-songs are usually anything but rhythmic, I tried to meet this challenge in 1972 with a new work to the Welsh text of the Communion Service, first called 'Cymun Bendigaid' but later *Offeren yn Arddull Canu Gwerin*, using folk-tunes. This had followed hot on the heels of the *Gelli Aur Variations*, which involved the tune *Llanymddyfri* and which I shared with other composers, Mervyn Burtch, Kenneth Gange and Leonard Pugh. Elwyn Jones of Carmarthen conducted the first performance with the Llandeilo School Orchestra and also tackled the 'folk mass' later for the Carmarthen National Eisteddfod.

For the Centenary of our College in 1972 I devised a programme for the BBC Welsh Orchestra which was entirely Welsh, in association with an old student, J Alwyn Jones of the BBC. As well as compositions by the five professors of music at Aberystwyth, we included music by the first Doctor of Music of the University of Wales, Richard Maldwyn Price (1890-1952), Arwel Hughes, David Harries and William Mathias. I had originally intended my Symphony No.3 to be called Concerto for String Quartet and Orchestra, but was told that a unified string quartet would never be available. As it turned out, of course, we had our own executants to play: Robert Jacoby, Leonard (Bill) James, Peter Kingswood and Geraint John. Kenneth Bowen and Carol Davies sang, and the leader of the orchestra, not as announced, turned out also to be an old student, David Llewelyn.

In Centenary Year we appointed Mansel Thomas as Honorary Professorial Fellow to the Music Department and gave the first performance of his new and vigorous Piano Quintet.

During May, June and July 1973, I contributed four short articles to *The Western Mail* on my philosophy, called 'Personal Column'. Cosmology has often exercised my mind.

Dr A B Thomas, who had helped me form the Music Club in 1952, reached his ninetieth birthday in September 1972 and he died in Aberystwyth the following year. The youngest of seven Carmarthen children, he had a contralto sister who was accompanist for the tours of Joseph Parry's *Blodwen* and *Arianwen*. He obtained a First in French at Aberystwyth in 1905 and went on to a doctorate in Lyons in 1910.

One of the most positive influences that we had in the Music Department, Aberystwyth, was Redvers Llewellyn, the distinguished operatic baritone, who died at the age of 73 in 1975. From 1956 he had taught singing and voice production for us. All the students, even the most timid, learnt how to 'present themselves'. Tom Redvers Llewellyn's impressive career included Carl Rosa, Sadlers Wells and Covent Garden; he was also Beecham's 'favourite' singer in Delius. A great optimist he said that experience could be divided into 'good' or 'bad'. Of the latter much could be converted to good, i.e. if you stubbed your toe, you said it was for good luck. Anything left — and there was very little — you called 'life'. I shall not easily forget his grim Iago's 'Credo' from *Otello* or the personally amusing 'Catalogue' song from *Don Giovanni*. I also enjoyed his lieder singing. When he retired from UCW he went on to part-time teaching — with exhausting commuting — at the Royal College of Music from 1969 until his death.

It was good to see our old friend, the third Lord Davies of Llandinam, elected chairman of the Welsh National Opera Company in December 1975. He was thus maintaining the active patronage of the arts that had been fostered by his great-aunts at Gregynog.

The Choral Society, thanks to Dr Cyril Williams, took part in a service in December 1976, which went out on the World Service of the BBC. In July of the following year I had the task of organising the music for the Installation of HRH The Prince of Wales as Chancellor of the University of Wales. The music before the ceremony proper included two items by Grace Williams, the important Welsh composer who had died earlier in the year. One of my first efforts in the early fifties had been to put on a performance of her *The Song of Mary*. This time it was part of *Castell Caernarfon* and a song, sung by Delyth Hopkins, *Midsummer Night*. In spite of at least one procession ignoring the marshall, I managed to get the right music coming to a suitable conclusion as His Royal Highness reached the dais. And it was gratifying that he had not forgotten his period as a student of Welsh and Welsh affairs. Glancing up from my score during the recessional, I was rewarded by a grin of recognition from Prince Charles.

One of our First Class students, Andrew Sidebottom, won a Maisie Lewis award from the Worshipful Company of Musicians and had the honour in May 1978 of giving an organ recital at Westminster Abbey. Later he took holy orders and is now a clergyman at St Mary's, Tenby, where another First Class student, John Harrison, recently awarded a PhD, is the organist.

We ran music festivals at Llanbadarn Church for a few years from 1978. This was largely due to the inspiration of the vicar, Canon Emrys Edwards, and it included the broadcasting of Mansel Thomas's Mass for mixed voices — and the following year, the celebration of the 900th anniversary of the completion of the Rhigyfarch Psalter.

In 1979 another festival, the Aberystwyth Festival, was started by the DBRW and, in spite of its concentration on frankly the light and popular, I was able to run a young composer's competition for three years. Dalwyn Henshall and Gareth Glyn shared the prize for a chamber work in 1980; Gareth Glyn won with his piano piece in 1981; and Howard Watt was commissioned to write a duet song in 1982. Now the Festival has been taken over by Ceredigion District Council.

Pauline Taylor was the guiding spirit behind the Enid Lewis memorial concert of October 1980, in which the music had ranged over many Welsh composers associated with UCW, from Maldwyn Price and Hubert Davies. Two outstanding pupils of Miss Lewis took part: Delme Bryn Jones and Gwawr Owen.

It seemed only too short a time when Miss Taylor, one-time member of the Dorian Trio and famous breeder of the Welsh cob stallion, Braint, herself passed on in June 1981.

From 1964, I decided that the students' 'Set Works' for study should include a Welsh composition each year. They were as follows:

1964-65	Grace Williams	*The Dancers*
1965-66	David Wynne	*Mosaic*, from *Suite of Three Pieces* (piano)
1966-67	David Harries	Violin Concerto, Op.18
1967-68	Alun Hoddinott	Divertimento for Wind Quartet
1968-69	Ian Parrott	Fantasy and Allegro
1969-70	Mansel Thomas	*Gwyn ap Nudd*
1970-71	Daniel Jones	Kettle Drum Sonata

1971-72	William Mathias	*St Teilo*
1972-73	Arwel Hughes	Fantasia in A minor for Strings
1973-74	Mansel Thomas	*Four Prayers from the Gaelic*
	Ian Parrott	*Flamingoes* (song)
1974-75	Trevor Roberts	*Pastoral*
1975-76	Robert Smith	*Pan Oeddwn Fachgen* (*A Dream of Youth*)
1976-77	Alun Hoddinott	Symphony No.2
	Alun Hoddinott	*Variants for Orchestra*
1977-78	Dilys Elwyn-Edwards	*Caneuon Natur* (three songs, 1977)
1978-79	Mansel Thomas	Mass for Mixed voices (1977)
1979-80	D Vaughan Thomas	*Saith o Ganeuon*
1980-81	David Wynne	*Chwe Chân i denor a thelyn* (1950)
1981-82	Alun Hoddinott	*Sinfonia Fidei*
1982-83	Grace Williams	*Sea Sketches*

Ian and Elizabeth at the British Music Information Centre, London, March 1986

Our external examiners have included H S Middleton, Edmund Rubbra, Gordon Jacob, Hans Redlich, Geoffrey Bush, Colin Kingsley and James Murray Brown. In the early days we shared them with Cardiff and Bangor, dropping them off in the south or taking tea in Dolgellau on the way to the north. Then Professor Hoddinott, on his appointment to the chair in Cardiff in 1967, decided that a single 'external' for the special requirements of his department should be appointed, so we went our different ways.

In my last years, the burden of office has been considerably lightened by the loyal and unstinting help of senior lecturer J Glynne Evans.

It might be mentioned that in a busy academic life, I also entertained many musical visitors from Canada, New Zealand, etc., and played *their* music in Aberystwyth.

Apart from many articles on other matters and reviews on Welsh events, I have written more specifically:

'Welsh Music from Within or Without', *The Welsh Anvil*, December 1954
'The Black Ram', *Dock Leaves*, May 1956
'Die Walisische Eisteddfod', *Musica*, July-August 1958
'Warlock in Wales', *The Musical Times*, October 1964
'The Music of William Mathias', *The Anglo-Welsh Review*, 1965.

I have also written MGG articles which have included those on David de Lloyd and Daniel Jones.

'Môr o gân yw Cymru i gyd' runs the saying. If Wales is full of singing — and enthusiastic singing, such as visitors do not suspect — you can find it in abundance by going to a service in a remote non-conformist chapel. No English church can give you attentive congregational participation of this quality — especially today when TV boggling has made people ignore or shrug off much that is of value in the civilised world.

Notes

[1]   *The Story of the Guild for the Promotion of Welsh Music*, a symposium [Angel Chambers, 94 Walter Road, Swansea, 1980]

[2]   See *The Western Mail*, October 2 1954, 'A Place in the World for Welsh Music'.

(d) *The Coventry Madonna and Bach*
by
Ian Parrott

Extract from *The Musical Times*, August 1959

After the bombing of 1940, a thirteenth-century painting of the Madonna and Child became visible high up on one of the walls of shattered Coventry Cathedral. This work of art had been obscured for years and was revealed by the unexpected sunlight. In discussion it is usually assumed that the painter must have intended that painting to be visible in the first instance. But has this always been the attitude of a religious artist?

The history of the Church has constantly shown the contrast of the hermit-like retreat from the world for private meditation and the mingling with fellow-creatures to do good. The two attitudes are not often wholly reconciled, and yet it seems that J S Bach has done perhaps more than any other great artist to show that these attitudes are not incompatible. His preface to the *Orgelbüchlein* is fairly frequently quoted but not so often understood: 'To the Honour of the Lord Most High, and that my neighbour may be taught thereby'. It is possible that the Coventry painter created his work of art primarily as a private act of worship, dedicating his painting to his Creator with no thought of human eyes. It is equally possible to argue that certain effects in medieval music which are not apparent to the listener are nevertheless relevant when considered in a religious light. The *canto firmo* in a motet by Dunstable may be unrecognizable as a melody in performance just as the underlying cruciform structure of a cathedral may not be taken in by the eye. Further devices such as an isorhythmic structure can have little significance to the listener but must have meant a great deal to the writer during the act of writing. We think so much of the finished product today that we do not always realize that the act of creation may have meant much more to the medieval mind, as it did in ancient civilizations, notably the Egyptians when they concealed metals inside bricks and when they hid certain foundation stones in a significant pattern which would never be seen in the future.

The importance of Bach's statement is in the dual purpose assigned to his compositions. Sometimes we can see him almost separating his two religious duties even when setting the same words. At a period in musical history when a key scheme was a measure of balance and common sense, he chose to deviate from the normal path as an act of private communion with his God. His listeners, performers and congregation alike, would wait with varying degrees of respect or boredom, while he launched into the words of *Et expecto resurrectionem mortuorum*. This passage, when it first occurs in the Mass in B minor, is like something out of this world — something which Bach alone was concerned to express as his thanksgiving. But after 23 bars of endlessly shifting ambiguities he comes back to earth with a paean of joy in D major, in which we hear him inviting the simple mortals of his congregation to join with him in worship. It seems that the first setting of the words is 'to the Honour of the Lord Most High' and the subsequent setting that his neighbour might benefit.

An objection will be raised here that an intelligent listener can get pleasure and even spiritual uplift from the first 'et expecto', so it will be interesting to examine examples of Bach's 'unheard' acts of devotion. Immediately to mind comes the device of writing the words of the Saviour in a different ink — a device which is additional to the heard device of giving Christ's passages in the St Matthew Passion a colouring of string tone. Also the diagonal pattern across the page of the entering and leaving instruments in the contralto recitative in the *Trauerode* is something extra and private on top of the heard effect of the imitation of a large number of bells in the orchestration.

We know that Bach frequently expected the listener to recall to mind the words of a hymn when the notes only were played by him in a chorale prelude. Yet, on the other hand, he would not expect them to know when he had put a sharp before a note to go with the word 'Cross'. More than anyone he seemed capable of adding something when he had already created an almost superhuman masterpiece. Perhaps one of his greatest achievements, although only one movement survives, is the powerful Cantata No.50, *Nun ist das Heil und die Kraft*. Its structure is grand and spacious. The voices, in eight parts, are divided antiphonally into two choruses: the fugal writing is masterly, and the independent instrumental parts are of great ingenuity, involving the 'joy' motif and the use of trumpets and drums.

I might hesitate here to give an example from this work where numbers are involved, since there has been so much obscure 'reading into' Bach's works, much as there has been in the case of Shakespeare; for example, the discoveries of the letters of the name Bacon by reading down the page, etc. There have recently been 'spoof' articles in many fields seeking to discredit the genuine inquirer, though it is known that Bach did enjoy musical anagrams, quodlibets and puzzle canons for their own sake: and when he represents the disciples' consternation at the prophecy that one of them will betray Jesus, the phrase 'Is it I?' occurs twenty-four times, sufficient for twice each. No audience is likely to start counting during the performance of the St Matthew Passion; this, therefore, is an 'unheard' effect. At the end of *Nun ist das Heil* there is a remarkable piece of construction, which is 'unheard' in detail, though its general implication will get through. In the last seven bars, the word 'day' occurs on a higher note than the word 'night' no fewer than twenty times. Anyone who has tried to write in eight 'real' vocal parts will know what a tussle it is to manipulate the parts at all, particularly as contrary motion is essential in order to avoid consecutive fifths and octaves. This truly is an example of devotion to the faith, as expressed in the words, which few composers before or since have had the fervour and technique to put into their work. It is the unheard part which is the equivalent of the unseen Madonna.

(e) An Introduction to Warlock
by
Ian Parrott

Extract from *The Peter Warlock Society Newsletter*, 1984

The editor asks for contributions on 'How I first came across Peter Warlock's music'. Arthur Hutchings' arresting article in the July 1984 Newsletter stimulates me to stir my stumps. Two ideas on his final page have provoked a reaction. "What you may or may not do with the third crochet" in Palestrina counterpoint reminds me that I was grilled by H K Andrews on this very point when having a go for some appointment at Oxford — I believe several amusing stories have circulated widely about Hutchings' own academic applications of a similar nature. The other word was Mangeot. When as a youngster I did in fact get the Margaret Bridges Scholarship to New College, Oxford, I had the pleasure of playing the viola in chamber music under André Mangeot's gentle soft-voiced instruction. More than anything else I remember his telling us where to put our fingers on the instrument — and the word 'finger' was always pronounced to rhyme with 'singer'.

New College, Oxford, proved to be the place where I fell under the spell of Peter Warlock, though, in fact, I remember a Mr Gardner at the prep school, Orley Farm, before that, who made the boys sing *What cheer? Good cheer!* — Ian Copley, I notice, just lifts that then newly-published unison song out of the commonplace. My teacher at Harrow, Reginald Thatcher, encouraged very little creativity in any way. Once when I showed him a new unfinished composition, he said: "I wouldn't finish it if I were you". Another memory of my schooldays is of a lazy violin teacher — and a lazy pupil. After one particular week, he said I had made considerable progress. As I knew only too well that I had not done a stroke of work, I found his remark strange to say the least.

Oxford, after a spell under the impressive direction of Sir Hugh Allen at the Royal College of Music, was an exciting change — again under the kindly influence of the Heather Professor, Sir Hugh Allen! Holding down two posts at once was more common then. But, in particular, I had the pleasure of knowing the professional college organist, Dr Sydney Watson. He also conducted the Harmonic Society, which had previously been directed by George Thewlis of Christchurch, a personal friend of Peter Warlock. Sydney Watson had two special enthusiasms: Glazunov (who died in 1936) and Warlock. For a time I showed an interest in Glazunov — and discovered that my wife's mother had known him — in particular, the rhythms of his sixth symphony. The sounds of Peter Warlock's harmonies meant even more to me, and before finishing my undergraduate days I had devised a concert, which involved getting the ladies of St Hugh's College to co-operate. My contemporary, Denis Mulgan, organ scholar of Worcester, helped, and we put on a varied programme at the ladies' college on May 30 1937, which included the three *Dirges*, then thought to be unperformable. Winifred Dussek sang the *Lillygay* cycle, and we included both *Sorrow's Lullaby* and *The Curlew* with Edward Manning, tenor, Frederick Wade, baritone, A E Smith, flute, and Elizabeth Kitson, cor anglais. The other performers were the Kirby String Quartet, the St Hugh's Choral Society and the Isis Orchestra, which gave *An Old Song* and also played my orchestration of the organ part for the solo version of *Bethlehem Down*. *Corpus Christi* was performed in the unaccompanied chorus version, with Mrs Dussek and Edward Manning as soloists. The evening ended in convivial fashion with *The Lady's Birthday*. The piano accompaniments for soloists were provided by myself and for choruses shared with Denis Mulgan and Robin Miller.

Humphrey Searle, then an undergraduate studying classics (he died in May 1982), gave us a friendly write-up, which made the whole enterprise seem most worthwhile. He obtained the lively interest of Constant Lambert and also wrote to Cecil Gray, who, though unable to attend, approved of our discreet muted string quartet support for the singers in parts of the *Dirges*. Apt, they were, for voices *with* viols.

In passing, it may be mentioned that St Hugh's had as Principal from 1886 to 1915 Miss C A E Moberly, who with her colleague, Eleanor Jourdain, visited Versailles in 1901 and 1902. Although I didn't know it at the time, later I was to be drawn back to St Hugh's when I wrote *The Music of 'An Adventure'* in 1966, dealing with the strange music heard at Versailles on the second visit.

And little did I know then that in 1950 I would settle in West Wales, only forty-five miles from Cefn Bryntalch, where Warlock wrote most of his greatest works. I thought often of the poems of Yeats with their references to the Irish curlew, but more often I travelled over 'the top' to Powys and the haunting cries of the Welsh curlew, which the composer had heard.

And then many of us responded happily to Pat Mills' advertisement to form a Society in 1963, and we have never looked back ...

Appendix 2

Programme to Celebrate the 80th Birthday of

IAN PARROTT

(March 5th 1996)

Alison Wells (soprano)
John Turner (recorder)
Keith Swallow (piano)

1 Songs: Ian Parrott
   I heard a Linnet courting (1940)
   Flamingoes (1972)
   Two Thoughtful Songs (1977)
     The fly
     Thee, God, I come from

2 *Aubade*, for recorder and piano (First Modern Performance)   Cyril Scott

3 *Aspects*, for piano (1975)   Ian Parrott

4 Songs: Peter Warlock
   Ha'nacker Mill
   Robin Good-Fellow
   The Fox
   Pretty Ring Time

5 *Songs of Renewal*, for soprano, recorder and piano (1995)   Ian Parrott
   (First Performance)

Interval

6 Humbert Wolfe Songs: Holst
   Persephone
   The Thought
   A Little Music
   Betelgeuse

7 Pieces for recorder and piano:
   Awel Dyfi (Scherzino) (1995) for solo recorder   Ian Parrott
      (First performance)
   Arabesque and Dance (1972)   Ian Parrott
   Mr Playford's Musical Banquet   David Cox

8 Piano Solos:
   In Smyrna   Elgar
   Rhapsody: *Westerham* (1940)   Ian Parrott

9 *Seascapes*, for soprano, recorder and piano   William Alwyn
     Dawn at Sea
     Seamist
     Song of the Drowned Man
     Black Gulls

Appendix 3

Diary of Events

1937 (age 21)
May 30:
   Conducted a concert of music by Peter Warlock at St Hugh's College, Oxford.

1939 (age 23)
August 17:
   Painted Sompting Church, near Lancing.

1940 (age 24)
March 31:
   Composed a theme in a dream (used later in finale of Symphony No.1).
December:
   Passed the examination for the degree of Doctor of Music, Oxford University.

1947 (age 31)
October 1:
   Appointed Lecturer in Music, Birmingham University.

1948 (age 32)
June - July:
   Conducted *The Bartered Bride* at Peter Jones, London.
December 20:
   Elected to the Executive Committee of the Composers Guild of Great Britain.

1950 (age 34)
July 19:
   Appointed to the Gregynog Chair of Music
   in the University College of Wales, Aberystwyth.

1951 (age 35)
September 5:
   Made a member of the Society for Psychical Research.
October:
   Elected a Vice-President of the Union of Graduates in Music.

1952 (age 36)
January:
   Listed in *The Music Book* [Hinrichsen] as a Representative Composer.
August 7:
   Conducted London Symphony Orchestra in *Luxor* at the National Eisteddfod, Aberystwyth.

1954 (age 38)
March:
   Made Chairman of the Guild for the Promotion of Welsh Music (held office until June 1956).
December:
   Subject of an article in *Grove's Dictionary of Music and Musicians*, Fifth Edition, Volume VI

1955 (age 39)
January:
   Elected District Member of the Council of the Incorporated Society of Musicians.

1956 (age 40)
April:
   Article on *The Black Ram* by Hans Redlich:
   'A New Welsh Folk Opera', *Music and Letters*

1957 (age 41)
July:
   Made a member of the Council of the Union of Graduates in Music.

1958 (age 42)
March 5:
   2-minute broadcast in Welsh in *Dyddiadur Cerdd*

1959 (age 43)
January:
   Photo as "Notable Teacher" in *A Course in Musical Composition Pt IV* (Norman Demuth) [Bosworth]
June 11 & 29:
   Took General Certificate of Education in Welsh, O level with oral proficiency (oral, grammar, dictation, unprepared translation and comprehension).

1961 (age 45)
March 25:
   Michael Parrott played Vivaldi's Cello Concerto No.5 with Mid-Wales Youth Orchestra conducted by Rae Jenkins, Parish Hall, Aberystwyth.
April 12:
   Presented to HM the Queen Mother.
July 1:
   Themes from Symphony No.1 arranged for two horns and performed in woods at Gregynog.

November 18:
: Subject of article by A F Leighton Thomas:
'A Many-sided Composer', *The Western Mail*

1962 (age 46)
July 19:
: Attended Buckingham Palace Garden Party with Elizabeth.

December:
: Appointed to the Executive Committee of the Incorporated Society of Musicians.

1962-1964: External Examiner for Bristol University

1963 (age 47)
April 20:
: Officially on the Executive Committee of the Guild for the Promotion of Welsh Music as well as being a Vice-President

May:
: On the Advisory Committee of the Peter Warlock Society
(with Gerald Cockshott, Ian Copley, Arnold Foster, Chris le Fleming, Tony Payne, Norman Gilbert, Frank Howes and Felix Aprahamian)

July:
: Composed quodlibet on *Nemo* for piano.

1964-1966: External Examiner for Manchester and Leicester Universities

1966 (age 50)
February:
: Musicology Award for the Year made by Harriet Cohen;
Presentation of medal: December 19

May 1:
: Descant on Dykes: tune to *Praise to the Holiest in the Height* (A&M 172) for use in TV Evensong from Llanbadarn, May 29

1970 (age 54)
May:
: Quoted on sleeve for *Rosemary Brown's Music*, Philips, 6500 049 [*LP*]
(Rosemary Brown and Peter Katin)

1971 (age 55)
November:
: Painting of *Brinkwells* by Elizabeth Parrott reproduced on sleeve of EMI, HQS1252 [*LP*]
(Elgar: Violin Sonata & String Quartet;
Hugh Bean, David Parkhouse, Music Group of London Quartet)

1979 (age 63)
November:
: *Aquarelle* referred to in repertoire by Jack Brymer in *The Clarinet*.

1980 (age 64)
December:
   Daniel Jones and Ian Parrott, Chapter IV in 'Welsh Orchestral Music, 1945-1970' submitted by Kevin Adams for PhD (Wales)

1983 (age 67)
December:
   Elizabeth Parrott's drawing of Henblas (the Parrott family home) reproduced on page 68 and *The Black Ram* referred to on page 164 of *Peterwell* (Bethan Phillips) [Gomer Press].

1984 (age 68)
December 10:
   Unveiled plaque to Peter Warlock at 30 Tite Street, London SW3.

Vice-Presidents of the Elgar Society at Malvern, June 4 1988
left to right: Jerold Northrop Moore, Ian, Christopher Robinson,
Percy Young, Michael Pope

1990 (age 74)
July 6:
   Listed in *Debrett's Distinguished People of Today*.

1991 (age 75)
February 24-28:
Portrait painted by Daphne Todd; exhibited at Coutts Gallery, November.

The portrait by Daphne Todd, 1991

1992 (age 76)
April 7:
Included in *Contemporary Composers* [St James Press] with commentary by Lyn Davies.

1996 (age 80)
March 12:
Visited Igor and Natasha Chroustchoff, son and daughter-in-law of Boris de Chroustchoff in the course of preparing the article 'Peter Warlock's *Away to Twiver* and His Honour Lionel Jellinek'
(see Appendix 6)

1999 (age 83)
May:
Played Chopin's Pleyel at the Villa Medici Giulini, Italy

Ian at the Villa Medici Giulini, May 1999

Appendix 4

Compositions

[NB: Bold type denotes published works and publishers' names]

Orchestral Works

Scherzo I in C (1933)
   Isis Orchestra: Oxford, June 1936
Fantasy for oboe, piano and strings (1935)
Malvern Music (1937)
   part of DMus composition
Malvern March (1938), for military band
De L'Estuaire à la Source, four movements for full orchestra (1939)
   originally for Liège competition, used for DMus composition
Russian Dance (1941), for small orchestra
   Farnborough Orchestra: July 1941
A Dream (1941), for small orchestra
   on theme composed in a dream and later used for finale of Symphony No.1;
   Farnborough Orchestra: July 1941
Scherzo II (1943)
   8 minutes;
   Modern Symphony Orchestra: December 1949
   (see also Symphony No.1, 2nd movement)
El Alamein, symphonic prelude for full orchestra (1944)
   [2121 4331 timp perc hp str]
   9-10 minutes; **Chester** (hire), 1946;
   Guildford Symphony Orchestra: October 1945;
   BBC Northern Orchestra conducted by Charles Groves: broadcast, October 23 1948;
   City of Birmingham Symphony Orchestra: February 12 1950, etc
   (see also Symphony No.1, 3rd movement)
Miniature Concerto for violin and small orchestra (1945)
   $12^1/_2$ minutes ["not too difficult!"]
Symphony No.1 (1946)
   I Preface (1946)   II Scherzo (1943)
   III *El Alamein* (1944)   IV Transition (1945)
   V Finale (1945)
   32 minutes ($3^1/_2 + 8 + 9 + 1^1/_2 + 9^1/_2$)

***Luxor*, symphonic impression for full orchestra** (1947)
[2222 4331 timp perc pf hp str]
15 minutes; **Lengnick** (hire), 1950;
awarded First Prize of the Royal Philharmonic Society, November 26 1949;
London Philharmonic Orchestra conducted by Sir Adrian Boult: London,
October 17 1950 (repeated Oxford, October 19 1950);
London Symphony Orchestra conducted by the composer: National Eisteddfod,
Aberystwyth, August 7 1952; etc

Piano Concerto (1948)
29-30 minutes (10 + 6 + 13)

***Pensieri*, concerto grosso for string orchestra** (1950)
16$^1/_2$ minutes; **Hinrichsen** (hire), 1954;
Wolverhampton, February 1952;
St Martin's, London, March 1953;
Birmingham, December 1959

Solemn Overture: *Romeo and Juliet* (1953; revised 1956)
[2222 4331 timp perc celesta hp str]
12-14 minutes; **Novello/Elkin** (hire), 1958;
awarded Bournemouth Symphony Orchestra Shakespeare Prize, May 9 1957;
Bournemouth Symphony Orchestra: Bournemouth, October 24 1957;
BBC Northern Orchestra conducted by George Hurst: broadcast, March 11 1958

Flourish for a Royal Visit (1955), for small orchestra
1$^1/_2$ minutes;
National Library of Wales in the presence of HM the Queen, August 8 1955

Orchestral Variations on a Theme of Dufay (*Se la face ay pale*) (1955)
[2222 2330 timp perc hp str]
12$^1/_2$ minutes; **Novello/Elkin** (hire), 1958

Suite of Four Shakespeare Dances (1956)

| [1] *Malcolm's March* | [2] *Juliet's Dump* |
| [3] *Sir Andrew's Galliard* | [4] *Katharina's Tarantella* |

[2222 4231 timp perc hp str]
12 minutes (4 + 3 + 2 + 3);
Novello/Elkin (hire), 1958;
National Youth Orchestra of Wales conducted by Clarence Raybould: 1962

Concerto for cor anglais and orchestra (1956)
Andante - con moto; Adagio; Presto
[2122 2210 timp perc hp str]
20 minutes (7 + 5 + 8); **Novello/Elkin** (hire), 1958;
Roger Winfield, Hallé Orchestra conducted by Sir John Barbirolli:
Cheltenham Festival, July 18 1958;
Leicester, February 1959

***Y Dair* (*The Three Ladies*)**
— **Gavotte, Sarabande and Scherzo on Welsh Folk-tunes** (1958)
[1] Gavotte: *Hen Ferchetan* (*Little Old Maid*)
[2] Sarabande for strings: *Mae Nghariad i'n Fenws* (*My Love's like Venus*)
[3] Scherzo: *Cwyn Mam Yng'Nghyfraith* (*The Mother-in-Law's Complaint*)
[2121 2210 timp perc hp str]
13 minutes (4 + 2 + 7);
Novello/Elkin (hire), 1959;
sarabande only, conducted by the composer: Gregynog, June 27 1959;
BBC Welsh Orchestra: broadcast in *Aclwyd y Gân* (BBC Wales),
(a) scherzo only (cut version - 4 minutes), conducted by Arwel Hughes: June 5 1958,
(b) gavotte only, conducted by the composer: April 10 1959,
(c) complete version, conducted by Rae Jenkins: recorded March 15 1961,
broadcast July 6 1961

Concert Overture: *Seithenin* * (1959)
[2222 4231 timp perc pf hp str]
8 minutes; **Novello/Elkin** (hire), 1959;
BBC commission;
BBC Welsh Orchestra conducted by Arwel Hughes: broadcast, December 11 1959;
London Philharmonic Orchestra conducted by Sir Adrian Boult and Wyn Morris: on tour, November 1964

Symphony No.2 (*Round the World*) (1960)
Allegretto - allegro con brio; Andante; Scherzando com memorie: allegro molto
[2222 4331 timp perc pf hp str]
110pp, 866 bars; 29 minutes ($9^1/_2 + 6 + 13^1/_2$);
Novello/Elkin (hire);
Sketched in USA and Canada and completed in New Zealand
— theme from 1st Movement arranged for piano duet; **B Brunton**, 1986

Concerto for cello and orchestra (1961)
Ritornello - Adagio - Allegro - Adagio (see also Fantasy for cello & piano, 1948);
Ritornello - Adagio - Ritornello
[2222 2210 timp perc pf celesta hp str]
13-14 minutes; **Novello/Elkin** (hire);
William Pleeth, Hallé Orchestra conducted by Sir John Barbirolli: Newtown, May 2 1963;
recorded by William Pleeth with the composer at the piano, June 14 1962

The Three Moorish Princesses (1964), for narrator and orchestra
[2121 2210 timp 2 perc str]
approx. 17 minutes; **Novello/Elkin** (hire);
on texts from *Stories from the Alhambra* by Iva Howard;
Leeds Symphonic Society: November 1966

March: *Broncastell* (1964), for concert band
[4 fl, picc, 2 ob, 4 cl, bass cl, 2 fag, 2 sax in E flat, 6 cornets (incl sop in E flat), 4 hrns in F, 2 baritones in B flat, 2 tbns in B flat, bass tbn, E flat bass, B flat bass, string bass, s-d, tri, glock, cym, bass drum and 3 timp]
rescored from piano piece of 1953; 4 minutes;
Yale University Concert Band Tour, 1965;
broadcast, BBC, June 29 1965

Suite for violin and orchestra (1965)
Introduction — *Wooden-legged Waltz*
Rhapsody (see also Rhapsody for violin and piano, 1958)
Bountiful Boogie (see also *Boogie* for violin and piano, 1965)
$8^1/_4$ minutes ($2^1/_4 + 3^1/_4 + 2^1/_4$);
commissiond by BBC Cardiff for TV *Auditorium*;
Colin Staveley, BBC Welsh Orchestra: broadcast, January 25 1968

Symphony No.3 (1966)
I Prelude   II Fantasia on a Chord in Tchaikovsky   III Rondo
[2121 2230 timp perc celesta hp str, with obbligato string quartet]
$17^1/_2$ minutes ($2^1/_2 + 7 + 8$);
BBC Welsh Orchestra: UCW Centenary, Aberystwyth, October 13 1972

Concerto for trombone and wind band (1967)
[2 fl, picc, 2 ob, 4 cl, bass cl, 2 fag, 2 alto sax, 3 cornets, 2 tpts, 4 hrns, 2 baritones, 2 tbns, 2 tubas, string bass, 2 perc (with optional cor anglais and baritone sax)]
adapted from Sonatina (1958); $7^1/_4$ minutes;
Musica Rara (trombone and piano version), 1968, re-issued 1985;
Yale University Concert Band Tour, 1968;
recorded by W Shepherd, USA, 1974

---

* The drunkard Prince of Dyfed who failed to guard the embankment for King Gwyddno of Cantre'r Gwaelod; on the night of a great feast the sea broke through, and the whole country, now Cardigan Bay, was flooded.

Fantasia on Welsh Tunes: *Land of Song* (1968)
[using *Braint, My Love is like Venus, Abergenny, David of the White Rock, Watching the Wheat, Braint* and *Abergenny* together, and *Aberystwyth*]
brass band; 8 minutes; **Boosey,** 1969;
test piece for Third Section Bands, Regional Qualifying Finals,
National Brass Band Championships, 1970

Homage to Two Masters (1970)
[2222 2334 perc timp pf str]
based on Bach and Elgar; 7 minutes;
London Repertoire Orchestra conducted by Ruth Gipps: November 21 1976

Harrow March (1970)
for Quatercentenary of Harrow School, July 6 1971; 4½ minutes
(also arranged for ten brass, 1984)

Reaching for the Light (1971)
[solo hpschd, pf, with 0201 2000 glockenspiel str]
dedicated to Sir George Trevelyan; 7½ minutes;
Attingham Park, August 21 1971;
Southampton University (conducted by Malcolm Davies), December 7 1973

Concertino for two guitars and small orchestra (1973)
[2121 0100 perc str]
10 minutes; Hornchurch, March 16 1974

Rumbustuoso Vernon*cello am* Griff*brett*
— variations on a theme of Vernon Griffiths for string orchestra (1974)
for the 80th birthday of Professor Vernon Griffiths, Christchurch, NZ;
recorded June 25 1974 for June 29

Sinfonietta (Symphony No.4) (1978)
Largo - Andante - Allegro
[2222 2200 timp perc str]
15½ minutes

Symphony No.5 (1979)
I Confrontation: *Largo - andante - allegretto*
II Alternation: *Allegretto - andante - con moto - andante - con moto*
III Integation: *Largo - andante - allegretto*
[2222 4231 timp 3 perc cel hp str]
27½ minutes (10½ + 9½ + 7½); **Lengnick;**
Birmingham Philharmonic Society conducted by Kenneth Page:
Coventry Cathedral, May 23 1981

Arfordir Ceredigion *(The Coast of Ceredigion)* (1992)
5 minutes; **Lengnick;**
commissioned by the National Eisteddfod;
BBC Welsh Orchestra: Aberystwyth, August 2 1992

Fanfare-Overture for a Somerset Festival (1993)
(7½)-8 minutes; **Lengnick;**
commissioned by Parrett Music Festival;
Southampton Youth Orchestra conducted by Keith Smith: Montacute,
July 3 & 10 1993, and (twice) at the Royal Festival Hall, London, in the same week;
recorded by Naxos, 1999

Prelude and Waltz for recorder and string orchestra (1997)
(waltz on a theme dreamed by Jeanne)
11 minutes; **Phylloscopus,** 2001;
Tenby, September 25 1998;
recorded by Olympia, 1999

Sinfonia Concertante (2003)
[1] *Reverie*   [2] *Ritornello*   [3] *Rhapsody*   [4] *Rondo*
recorder, solo violin, string orchestra and percussion; 18 minutes

Above and opposite: *Fanfare-Overture*, a passage from the autograph score

Reproduced by kind permission of Alfred Lengnick & Co [a division of Complete Music Ltd].
Materials available to hire from Chester Music.

Chamber Music

Organ Sonata (1933)
  (see also *Agincourt*, 1948)
Foursome for eight hands and two pianos (1935: completed 1939)
  8 minutes
Oboe Sonata (1935/1936) (later a Concerto)
  in three movements
Minuet for oboe and piano (1935)
  second movement of above; $3\frac{1}{2}$ minutes; **Schott**, 1950;
  Oxford, November 1936;
  Denis Mulgan: broadcast, December 9 1949
Piece for violin and piano (1937)
  for May and Michael Crum
Trio for flute, violin and piano (1937)
  11 minutes
Nocturne (1937), for piano
  $3\frac{1}{2}$ minutes
The Malvern Hills (1938), for piano
Betinka, romance for piano (1939)
  4 minutes; **Paterson**, 1940
Westerham, rhapsody for piano (1940)
  4 minutes; **Lengnick**, 1948; several performances
Fuga Giocosa (1942), for piano
Berceuse for string quartet (1942)
  $4\frac{1}{2}$ minutes (see also String Quartet No.1)
Impromptu (1942), for piano
Theme and Six Variants for piano (1945)
  $12\frac{1}{2}$ minutes; **Lengnick**, 1947;
  Iris Loveridge: St Bartholomew the Great, London, October 17 1946;
  Marjorie Blackburn: broadcast, BBC Midland, November 25 1949;
  Eunice Eaton: Town Hall, New York, April 20 1950, etc
String Quartet No.1 (1945/1946)
  in three movements using *Berceuse* (1942) as second movement;
  originally called Three Pieces for String Quartet;
  18 minutes ($6 + 4\frac{1}{2} + 7\frac{1}{2}$);
  CPNM, London, May 2 1950;
  finale broadcast: January 19 1953
Duet for two flutes unaccompanied (1946)
  in three movements; 8 minutes;
  Ann and Marcus Holmes: St Bartholomew the Great, London, 1946
Fantasy and Allegro for two pianos (1946)
  11 minutes; **Lengnick**, 1947;
  Kathleen Cooper and Dorothea Vincent: Wigmore Hall, London, May 1 1947;
  broadcast, BBC London (Contemporary British Composers), December 30 1947, etc
Oboe Quartet (1946)
  in three movements; c14 minutes ($4\frac{1}{2} + 3\frac{3}{4} + 3\frac{1}{4}$);
  Chester (hire), 1955;
  Denis Mulgan (oboe): Balliol College, Oxford, October 19 1947;
  Edward Selwyn and Masters Trio: broadcast, BBC London, November 13 1948
Wind Quintet No.1 (1948)
  in three movements; $12\frac{1}{2}$ minutes;
  Birmingham, May 6 1949

Agincourt, pastoral and epic for organ (1948)
   8 minutes; partly based on material from Organ Sonata (1933)
Fantasy for cello and piano (1948)
   7 minutes;
   Norman Jones: Birmingham, October 8 1948;
   Gwendolen McGill, London, November 27 1952
Aquarelle for clarinet and piano (1948)
   also for viola and piano; $5^1/_2$ minutes; **Chester,** 1952;
   Aberystwyth, 1951
Fantasy-trio for violin cello and piano (1950)
   13 minutes;
   International Trio: RBA Galleries, London, May 24 1951
Scherzo: *Hobos Riding* (1951)
   oboe, oboe d'amore, cor anglais and heckelphone; 4 minutes;
   for the London Oboe Quartet (S Sutcliffe, D Bridger, P Newbury, J MacGillivray)
Dafydd y Garreg Wen (1951), for viola and piano
   $10-10^1/_2$ minutes;
   Raymond Jeremy: Aberystwyth, October 1951
Three Pieces for piano: *Gosteg, Profiad & Caniad* (1951)
   $5^3/_4$ minutes ($1^1/_2 + 1^1/_4 + 3$)
The Birds of Glanyrafon (1953), for piano
   $1^3/_4$ minutes; to Mrs Ruth Dugdale
Broncastell (1953), for piano
   $1^3/_4$ minutes; to Peggy and Jack Challinor
   — also extended and scored for brass band; 4 minutes
   (see also *Broncastell* for concert band, 1964)
Three Welsh Airs for two recorders and piano (or harp) (1954)
   Dygan Caersws; Hoffedd Hywel ab Owain Gwynedd; Dadl Dau
   $3^1/_4$ minutes ($1 + 1^3/_4 + ^1/_2$); **Schott,** 1955
By the Ystwyth (1954), for piano
   $2^1/_2$ minutes; to Myfanwy Jones
Little Fugato for piano (1954)
   $2^1/_2$ minutes; to David Harries
String Quartet No.2 in G sharp (1955)
   Ritornello: adagio - Andante con dolore - Tempo di Menuetto quasi ritornello - Allegro agitato - Ritornello: adagio
   $15^1/_2$ minutes ($1^1/_2 + 4 + 3^1/_4 + 4^3/_4 + 1^1/_4$):
   Swansea, 1956;
   J Rooper Prize, 1983
Family Prelude & Fugue for strings and piano (1956)
   (children) violin 1 easy, cello easy, viola optional;
   violin 2 open strings added, 1957; piano part revised, 1958;
   $3^1/_2$ minutes ($1^1/_2 + 2$); **Chester,** 1958;
   several performances
Capriccio for trumpet and piano (1956)
   $3^1/_2$ minutes;
   Aberystwyth, November 1956; Swansea, July 1957, etc
Ceredigion, **three pieces with interludes for harp solo** (1957)
   8 minutes; **Gwynne (University of Wales Press),** 1962;
   Ann Griffiths: Israel, September 1959;
   Vera Dulova: Moscow Philharmonic Society, November 15 1963;
   also performed and recorded in the USA by Phyllis Schlomovitz, 1970
String Quartet No.3 (1957)
   Andante ; Allegretto leggiero

16 minutes (5 + 11);
London String Quartet: Bangor, May 1961
Elegy for organ (1958)
2½ minutes; to Peter Boorman
Rhapsody for violin and piano (1958)
3¼ minutes; to Jelly d'Aranyi
(see also *Boogie* for violin and piano, 1965)
Sonatina for trombone and piano (1958)
Allegretto; Allegro con brio
6½ minutes (3¼ + 3¼); to Alun Hoddinott;
Barry, Glamorgan, January 20 1959
Fantasy for James Blades (1959)
[tri, cym, tam-tam, glock, xylo, vibra, 2 timp, side-drum, attd cymb & foot bass drum]
approx. 3 minutes
Blackbird Piece (1960)
flute (and piccolo), oboe, clarinet, horn, bassoon and piano; 2¾-3 minutes;
based on a blackbird heard in May 1955;
dedicated to the Bournemouth Wind Ensemble;
Aberystwyth, February 22 1960
Three Easy Pieces for piano (1961)
[1] *A Walk through the Farmyard*
[2] *Three Girls and a Boy*
    "For Diana, Celia, Edward & Sonia from Uncle Ian"
[3] *On the Escalator*
printed in *Music Teacher*, February and June 1970
Toccata for organ (1962)
4½ minutes; **Novello/Elkin**, 1965;
Peter Boorman: St Johns College, Cambridge, May 13 1962
Septet (1962)
Adagio - allegretto con moto; Adagio - lento; Adagio - allegretto con spirito
15 minutes (4 + 4¼ + 6¾);
commissioned by the Guild for the Promotion of Welsh Music;
Virtuoso Ensemble: Cheltenham Festival, July 10 1962; Llanelli, August 10 1962
String Quartet No.4 (1963)
Preface: *allegro;* Lento dolce; *Allegro con fuoco;* Lento dolce; Epilogue: *allegro leggiero*
13½ minutes (½ + 4 + 6 + 1½ + 1½); **Griffiths**, 1999;
Aberystwyth Ensemble, September 1964;
Allegri Quartet: Wigmore Hall, London, May 1966;
recorded by University Ensemble of Cardiff for Lyrita, July 1971
Fantasy for piano (1965)
5½ minutes; **B Brunton**, 1986
David Harries: Bangor, March 8 1965; Colin Kingsley: Birmingham, October 11 1965
Boogie (1965), for violin and piano
3 minutes; to be paired with *Rhapsody* (1958) as *Rhapsody and Boogie*
Abergenny (1965), for crwth with optional clarinet
1½ minutes; for Yvonne Cousins
Big Hat Guy (1965)
violin (easy, Grade 3) and piano; 2¼ minutes;
for the *D Roger Jones Memorial Volume*; **GPWM**, 1972
Partita on two Welsh tunes for harp (1967)
[*Braint* and *Abergenny*]
8 minutes; **Lloyd Davies, Gilwern (Adlais)**;
commissioned by Ann Griffiths;
Ann Griffiths: St Davids Cathedral, July 11 1967

Pant Glas, idyll for violin, glockenspiel and piano (1967)
   4$^1/_2$ minutes
Mosaics (1968), for organ
   8 minutes;
   Rodney Baldwyn: Pershore Abbey, June 22 1969
Four Silhouettes for solo flute (1969)
   [MER, JOS, GAB, CLA]
   3$^1/_2$ minutes;
   Claire Polin: Aberystwyth, May 21 1969
Two Dances for flute and harp (1969)
   8$^1/_2$ minutes; "for Claire & Phyllis"; **GPWM**, 1985
Wind Quintet No.2 (*Fresh about Cook Strait*) (1970)
   13$^1/_4$ minutes; written in New Zealand;
   Phylloscopus, 1999;
   commissioned by BBC Cardiff: recorded March 3 1971, broadcast May 14 1971;
   Bromsgrove Festival, April 29 1971
Homage to Two Masters, re-arranged for organ (1971)
   for Rodney Baldwyn;
   Jennifer Bate: Swansea Festival, October 15 1974
   [see orchestral works; also Suite No.1 for organ (1977)]
Arabesque and Dance for treble recorder and harpsichord (1972)
   or flute and piano; 2$^3/_4$ minutes (1$^1/_4$ + 1$^1/_2$); **Thames/Wm Elkin**, 1990;
   Malcolm Davies: 1972
Soliloquy and Dance for harp (1973)
   3$^1/_4$ minutes (1$^1/_4$ + 2); **Thames/Wm Elkin**, 1974;
   Susan Drake: Swansea Festival, October 15 1974
Fanfare and March (1973), for two trumpets, trombone and bass tuba in E flat
   4$^1/_4$ minutes; **EMI**, 1976;
   October 1973
Devil's Bridge Jaunt (1974), for cello and piano
   4$^1/_4$ minutes (3 minutes without repeat); **GPWM**, 1979
Fantasia for organ (1974)
   9 minutes;
   commissioned by BBC Cardiff; March 4 1975
Aspects (1975), for piano
   14 minutes; **B Brunton (Oecumuse)**, 1986;
   Elisabeth Klein: Copenhagen, March 12 1976; Aberystwyth, October 1976;
   Oslo, September 1 1977
Gleaming Brass (1976), for two trumpets, horn, trombone and tuba
   6 minutes; originally called *Polished Brass*; **EMI**, 1977
Duo Fantastico No.1 (1976), for violin and piano
   7$^1/_2$ minutes; for Erich Gruenberg;
   Erich Gruenberg and John McCabe: 1981
Suite No.1 for organ (1977)
   Paean of Praise; *Prayer for Peace*; *Homage to Two Masters* (see version of 1971)
   13 minutes (3$^1/_2$ + 2$^1/_2$ + 7); **Oecumuse**, 1982;
   Andrew Sidebottom: Westminster Abbey, London, June 1 1978;
   Jennifer Bate: St George's, Hanover Square, London, May 17 1984
Rhapsody for trumpet and organ (1977)
   4 minutes; **Oecumuse**, 1983;
   Bram Wiggins and Jennifer Bate: Haverfordwest, November 11 1978
Arfon, **suite for harp** (1978)
   in five movements; 10 minutes;

Arfon, page one of the autograph

commissioned by Elinor Bennett; **Curiad**, 1996;
Elinor Bennett: North Wales Festival, St Asaph, September 27 1978
Fantasy-Sonata for clarinet and piano (1979)
14$^1/_2$ minutes; **Thames/Wm Elkin**, 1982; re-issued in *Woodwind Library*, 1987;
commissioned by the Welsh Arts Council for performance by Academi St Teilo;
Alun Cooper and Gerald Jones: Carmarthen Arts Club, December 6 1979;
Keith Wilson: Yale, USA, October 1986
Hands Across the Years (in memoriam Gerald Finzi) (1980), for organ
10 minutes;
Jennifer Bate: Harrogate Festival, August 8 1983
Reflections for violin and piano (1982)
8 minutes; dedicated to Leonard James;
Leonard James: 1983
Suite for cello and piano (1982)
   STEFANergico: *andante - allegro energico*; LOLArgo: *largo*;
   NICCOLO: *capriccioso e nicchiaremente (Allegro)*;
   DIMinuendo: *allegretto, un poco maestoso (Dygan Caersws)*;
   accALEXANDERando: *allegro non troppo - piu mosso*
12$^1/_2$ minutes (2 + 3 + 2$^1/_2$ + 1$^1/_2$ + 3$^1/_2$);
dedicated to Stefan Popov;
Nicholas Jones and Gayle Light: Purcell Room, London, February 5 1985
Duo for clarinet and trumpet (1983)
5 minutes; for Alan Hacker and Bram Wiggins;
St George's, Hanover Square, London, May 17 1984
Autumn Landscape (1983), for oboe and piano
6$^1/_2$ minutes; **Thames/Wm Elkin**, 1987;
David Cowley and Gordon Back: broadcast, BBC Radio 3, March 6 1986,
Marcia Ferran: broadcast, Sydney, Australia, January 1994
Kaleidoscope ('Page after Page') (1985), for piano trio
10 minutes; Leicester, January 21 1987
Suite No.2 for organ (1986)
12 minutes; **Oecumuse**, 1986;
commissioned by Malcolm Watts: St David's Cathedral, July 22 1986
Duetto for violin and viola (1986)
15 minutes
Fun Fugato & Awkward Waltz (1987), for bassoon and piano
5 minutes; **Thames/Wm Elkin**, 1990
Bridal Procession for organ (1988)
2 minutes; for Ceri Harries and Christine Edwards
Duo for two guitars (1988)
Prelude; Boogie; Interlude; March; Postlude
11 minutes; **Berben, Ancona**, 1989;
commissioned by Frances Griffin and Leo Turner:
Birmingham Arts Centre, November 6 1988
Duo Fantastico No.2 (1990), for violin and piano
9 minutes;
Leonard James and Lyn Davies: Aberystwyth, March 9 1991
Humoresque (1993), for piano
4 minutes;
in *British Contemporary Music Anthology*, 1996-7 [Frontier Press]
Three North Wales Tunes for two guitars (1993)
A Wrexham Pipe-Dance; Llangollen Bards; The Men of Machynlleth
2 minutes (30+45+45 sec);
from *Alawon fy Ngwlad* by Nicholas Bennett, Newtown, 1896

Fantasising on a Welsh Tune (*Dygan Caersws*) (1993)
   Allegro - tempo di valse andante - allegro vivo - allegretto con moto
   flute, oboe and piano (or violin, cello and piano);
   8 minutes; **Griffiths Edition**, 1995;
   for the Oriel Trio (Philip Gammon, piano; Betty Mills, flute; Richard Weigall, oboe)

String Quartet No.5 (Divertimento) (1994)
   Purposeful Prelude: andante - allegro - ; Hopeful Hymn: adagio non troppo;
   Rumba Rondo: allegro con moto
   11 minutes; for Alan and Betty Harries' Golden Wedding, May 5 1995;
   Llanbadarn, June 8 1996

Awel Dyfi, **scherzino for solo recorder** (1995)
   2 minutes; **Forsyth**, 1997;
   John Turner: Machynlleth Tabernacl, March 5 1996

Happiness, melodrama for reciter and recorder (1995)
   6 minutes; for David Cox's 80th birthday, February 4 1996

The Wrexham Pipers meet the Machynlleth Marchers (1996)
   recorder and guitar; 4 minutes;
   based on two tunes in *Alawon Ty Ngwlad* by Nicholas Bennett, Newtown, 1896;
   John Turner and Craig Ogden: Halifax, November 7 1996

Farewell to David (1997), for recorder and piano
   3 minutes; for Memorial Concert for David Cox, Purcell School, May 25 1997

Portraits **for recorder and piano** (1999)
   I Jack Moeran   II Gerald Finzi   III Leonard James
   IV David Cox   V William Mathias   VI Postlude
   21 minutes; **Phylloscopus**, 1999;
   Bangor, November 4 1999

An Old Tyrley Shepherd Song (1999), for organ
   3$^1/_2$ minutes; **Thames/Wm Elkin**, 1990;
   Malcolm Rudland: Great Warley, May 29 1999

Rondo Giocoso **for bassoon and piano** (1999)
   6$^1/_2$ minutes; **Phylloscopus**, 1999;
   Graham Salvage: Gatley, October 5 1999

Duo for recorder and cello (2001)
   Cock-crow; Irregular Interlude; Jiggery-fuguery
   6$^1/_2$ minutes;
   John Turner and Jonathan Price: Stockport Grammar School, October 5 2002

Dialogue and Dance for recorder and organ (2002)
   6 minutes; **Peacock Press**, 2003;
   John Turner and David Gibbs: Carlisle Cathedral, July 15 2002

Miscellaneous early works in MS (1926-1935)
   including numerous sonatas and other pieces for piano, *Siberian March* (1928),
   Spanish Dance (1934) and Flute Sonatina (1935)

Choral Works

Two Nature Pieces for chorus and orchestra (1936/1937)
    BMus exercise
Lament for the Death of Ghengis Khan (1938)
    unaccompanied; 4 minutes; part of DMus composition
Jolly Good Ale and Old (1939)
    male voices; 1½ minutes; **Novello/Elkin**, 1946
Anthem: Earth Rejoices (1939)
    3 minutes; **Weekes**, 1946
Psalm 91 (1946), for bass, chorus and orchestra
    15-17 minutes; **Lengnick**, 1949;
    Belfast Philharmonic Society: March 1951; Gregynog, June 1956
All the Woods Answer (1949)
    [from *Epithalamium* by Edmund Spenser]
    unaccompanied voices; 5½ minutes
Two songs from *Voices in a Giant City* by A S J Tessimond (1949)
    [1] **Money Talks**
    male voices; 4 minutes; **Novello/Elkin**, 1951;
    Eisteddfod, Aberystwyth, 1952; Llanidloes, September 1955;
    Singers in Consort: broadcast, January 1956
    [2] **Song in a Saloon Bar**
    male voices and piano; 4¼ minutes;
    Gwynn (University of Wales Press) (Curwen), 1963;
    Llanidloes, September 1955, etc.;
    — also version for male voices with brass and percussion (1968):
    Queen Elizabeth Hall, London, May 19 1968
Nativity Cantata: *Three Kings Have Come* (1951)
    [words: Flecker]
    female voices or SATB with soprano and baritone soli, piano and strings; 25 minutes;
    Letchworth (conducted by Hans Redlich), May 17 1952;
    Cambridge (conducted by Allan Percival), November 22 1952
    (see also Carol, 1964)
Carol Plygain (1957)
    [geiriau Huw Morus]
    SATB; 1½ minutes; **Gwynn (University of Wales Press) (Curwen)**, 1963;
    Llanbadarn Fawr Church, December 1957
Y Dylanwad (*The Divine Influence*) (1957)
    [words: Islwyn]
    SATB and organ; 4½ minutes
Magnificat & Nunc Dimittis (1961)
    trebles and organ; in Welsh and English; approx. 7-8 minutes;
    — revised version commissioned by Malcolm Watts, St David's Cathedral;
    two-part trebles with organ; 10 minutes (5 + 5); **Oecumuse**, 1987
Cantata: *Jubilate Deo* (1963)
    21 minutes;
    Llanbadarn Fawr Church, March 4 1968;
    Arts Council, London (solo voices with piano), October 20 1967
Carol: *Three Kings Have Come* (1964)
    [Welsh words by Sir T H Parry-Williams]
    based on Nativity Cantata, 1951; 3 minutes
Adam Lay Ybounden (1964)
    unison with piano or organ; 1½ minutes; **Oecumuse**, 1990;
    rejected by Elizabeth Poston for *The Cambridge Hymnal*, October 1964;
    recorded: Sydney, Australia, MBS 256D, January 25 1992

The Song of the Stones of St Davids (1968)
[words: Nancy Thomas]
SATB and organ; 3³/₄ minutes; **Samuel King**, 1994;
recorded: Horizon, in *Contemporary Welsh Choral Music*, June 1969
Offertory Motet: *Diffusa est gratia in labiis tuis* (1968)
ATBB; 2 minutes; for James Griffett;
Pro Cantione Antiqua: Purcell Room, London, March 20 1969
Welsh Folk Song Mass (*Offeren yr Arddull Canu Gwerin*) (1972)
[originally *Cymun Bendigaid*]
voice (or voices) [a] with organ or piano
[b] with guitar and percussion band (2 requintos, 4 guitars, bass [rebec], 2 percussion);
17¹/₂ minutes; **Thames/Wm Elkin**, 1973;
performed with organ, Rowland Jones: Bangor, December 12 1973
Song for Dyfed (1973), for two narrators, chorus and piano
15 mins;
commissioned by Côr Dyfed with funds provided by the Welsh Arts Council;
Côr Dyfed conducted by John Davies: Lampeter, 1975
Introit: *Surely the Lord is in this Place* (1974)
SA in three parts; 3 minutes; **Oecumuse**, 1977;
commissioned for the Centenary of All Saints, Llanelli, and dedicated to AFLT;
Llanelli, September 22 1974
Funeral Rite Text & Rite of Baptism of Children (1975)
voices, 2 guitars, percussion and/or organ; written for ICEL
Master Hugues of Saxe-Gotha (an Unknown Musician) (1975)
[words: Robert Browning]
male voices and piano; 3 minutes;
— revised for SATB and piano (1987) and published **B Brunton**, 1987;
London Welsh Choral conducted by Kenneth Bowen: June 18 1988
Cymru Fach (1976)
[words from Eifion Wyn, 1908, and Hen Benillion No.486, Sir T H Parry-Williams, 1956]
male voices unaccompanied; 5 minutes;
commissioned by North Wales Arts Association for the Brythoniaid Male Voice Choir
My Cousin Alice (1982)
[words: Jane Wilson]
mezzo-soprano, tenor, chorus, piano and tape of birds (c28+28+20 seconds);
3 minutes; **Banks**, 1984;
UCW, Aberystwyth, May 16 1983
Anthem of Dedication (James I 17 & Liturgy) (1985)
4¹/₂ minutes; **Oecumuse**, 1985;
service, Llanbadarn Fawr, October 20 1985
Mae 'Nghariad i'n Fenws (1987)
new version arranged for SATB and baritone solo;
2 minutes; **B Brunton (Oecumuse)**, 1987
Carol: *The Christ Child* (1987)
[words: Barbara Bonner-Morgan]
SATB with piano or organ; 4¹/₂ minutes; **Oecumuse**, 1987;
New Oxford Singers: Savoy Chapel, London, December 3 1987;
— version with orchestra (1988): [2121 2210 timp perc str];
recorded by Royal Liverpool Philharmonic Society, 1999;
— version with brass band (1993)
Arglwydd Ein Iôr Ni (1991)
SSATB unaccompanied; 5 minutes;
Gwynn, 1993;
Lower Machen Festival (conducted by Royston Havard), June 30 1991

Percyisms (2000), for soprano, mixed chorus, recorder, cello and harpsichord
A melodrama for the 90th birthday of Dr Percy Marshall Young, with apologies to Handel, Shelley, O'Shaughnessy, Elgar, Lewis Carroll and both Gilbert and Sullivan
5 minutes;
Elizabeth Atherton, The John Powell Singers, John Turner, Jonathan Price and Janet Simpson: The Barbirolli Room, Bridgewater Hall, Manchester, May 11 2002

Songs

I heard a Linnet Courting (1940) [words: Robert Bridges]
$2^1/_2$ minutes; **Lengnick**, 1948;
several performances; recorded Paraclete (USA), 1946
Four Songs of Absence (1942-1944)
   [1] *O Mieli Moy* (*O Dearest One*) (1942) [from Mikhail Lermontov's *The Novice*]
   [2] *Wie dir, so mir* (1942) [words: Justinus Kerner]
   [3] ***Absence*** (1943) [words: John Donne]
   GPWM, 1991;
   [4] *How Many Times do I Love Thee?* (1944) [words: Thomas Lovell Beddoes]
9 minutes $(1 + 2^1/_2 + 3 + 2^1/_2)$;
Mollie Sands: Wigmore Hall, London, December 1 1948
In Phaeacia (1945) [words: James Elroy Flecker]
5 minutes; **Lengnick**, 1948; broadcast, Sophie Wyss: BBC, London, March 1950
(see also *Two Flecker Settings* below)
Two Flecker Settings (1945-1946) [words: Flecker]
for high voice, oboe, clarinet and string orchestra
   [1] *In Phaeacia* (1945)
orchestration of the above;
   [2] *A Ship, an Isle, a Sickle Moon* (1946)
9 minutes (5 + 4); **Lengnick** (hire)
Gregynog and Aberystwyth, November 1954
Leaves (1948) [words: Elizabeth Ward, aged 11]
$2^1/_2$ minutes; **Lengnick**, 1949;
Sophie Wyss: broadcast, BBC, London, March 6 1950
A Child's Hunting Song (1954), for soprano, flute and piano
[words from the 7th century Welsh of Gododdin by Sir H Idris Bell]
Swansea, December 1960
Flamingoes (1972) [words: Jane Wilson]
$4^3/_4$ minutes; **Thames/Wm Elkin**, 1973
Three Thoughtful Songs (1977), for high voice
   [1] ***The Fly*** [words: William Blake, 1789]
   B Brunton (Oecumuse), 1988;
   [2] *Song for the Wind* [words: Jane Wilson, 1977]
   [3] ***Thee, God, I come from*** [words: Gerard Manley Hopkins, 1885]
   B Brunton (Oecumuse), 1988;
5 minutes $(1^3/_4 + 1^1/_2 + 1^3/_4)$;
Ruth Allsebrook with James Murray Brown: UCW, Aberystwyth, May 16 1983;
Kenneth Bowen with Paul Hamburger: broadcast, BBC Radio 3, December 8 1982
No Complaints, song cycle (1984), for medium voice and piano
   [1] Prelude   [2] Ritornello [from poem by Edward Bowen]
   [3] *The Psycho-Analyst* [words: A S J Tessimond]

[4] Reverie [from poem by Dora L Bowen, 1955]
[5] Ritornello [from poems by Walt Whitman]
[6] Interlude   [7] *Advice to a Young River* [poem by Jane Wilson, 1983]
[8] *Humble Men* [from Ecclesiasticus] (see also *Eastern Wisdom* below)
[9] *Bees* [poem by Lo Yin, 833-909] (see also *Eastern Wisdom* below)
[10] Ritornello [reprise of words from No.2, etc]
20 minutes; commissioned by Lyn Davies with funds from the Welsh Arts Council;
Lyn Davies and Richard Simm: St David's Hall, Cardiff, March 4 1986

Eastern Wisdom, **song cycle with small orchestra** (1987)
[1] Prelude   [2] *Bees* (orchestration of *No Complaints*, No.9)
[3] *Humble Men* (orchestration of *No Complaints*, No.8)
[4] *He Comes* [from Tagore, *Gitanjali* (song offerings), Nos. 45 and 101]
11½ minutes (3 + 1¼ + 2½ + 4¾);   **B Brunton (Oecumuse)**, 1988
— also version of *He Comes* with piano accompaniment (1987)

Song of Joy (1988) [words: W H Davies]
3 minutes; **Oecumuse**, 1990;
for Evelyn Nicholson

Barden Fell (1988) [words: Jane Wilson]
voice and oboe; 2 minutes

Aphorisms and Arias of Death and Life (1995) [texts various]
cycle for soprano, baritone and piano; 20 minutes;
Elen ap Robert (sop), Jeremy Huw Williams (bar), Iwan Llewellyn Jones (pno);
North Wales Music Festival, St Asaph, September 18 1996

The 80th Birthday Concert, Machynlleth, March 5th 1996
left to right: Margaret & John Turner, Alison Wells, Ian, Jeanne

Songs of Renewal (1995), for soprano, recorder and piano
7 minutes;
Alison Wells, John Turner, Keith Swallow: Machynlleth Tabernacl, March 5 1996
Meditation on *Llansannan* (1997), for voice and piano
4 minutes; for Jeremy Huw Williams;
Great Hall, Aberystwyth, December 11 1997
Paraphrases for Wilfrid (2002)
recorder, soprano and optional guitar; 5½ minutes

Opera and Ballet

The Sergeant-Major's Daughter, burlesque opera (1942-1943)
Cairo: 276 Wing, Heliopolis, July 8 1943;
63 General Hospital, Helmich, July 20 1943; 'Music for All', July 1943;
accepted by BBC, August 1945 (later rejected); accepted by NODA, January 1947
— overture, new version for theatre orchestra (1944):
Birmingham School of Music Orchestra: March 20 1950
Maid in Birmingham, ballet [suite] (1949)
23-26 minutes;
broadcast, BBC Midland, January 1951
The Black Ram, opera in a prologue and two acts (1951-1953)
[libretto by Sir H Idris Bell; Welsh version by Sir Thomas Parry-Williams]
2 hours; **Gwynn (University of Wales Press) (Curwen)**, vocal score, 1957;
overture and prologue only: Aberystwyth, November 30 & December 1 1952;
dances, Aberystwyth Players: broadcast, BBC Wales, February 1 1954;
overture only: broadcast, BBC Wales, June 23 1954;
concert version in Welsh (conducted by Arwel Hughes): broadcast, February 28 1957, and recording repeated (1 hour extract), BBC Overseas Service, March 1 1958;
staged version: Aberystwyth, March 9, 10 & 11 1966;
— version of overture for large orchestra (1953)
Hallé Orchestra conducted by Sir John Barbirolli: Newtown, May 13 1954, and Wolverhampton, November 10 1954
Once Upon a Time
(or *The Wife who liked Fairy Tales*), comic opera in one act (1958-1959)
[libretto by Cecil Price]
soprano, tenor, baritone and piano; 40 minutes;
Marie Sutherland, Edmund Bohan, Winston Sharp, Michael Toovey (piano): Christchurch, New Zealand, December 3 1960;
Amanda Williams, Kenneth Bowen, Redvers Llewellyn, Charles Clements (piano): Aberystwyth, April 4 1961
Eirioes T Jones, Kenneth Bowen, Redvers Llewellyn, Charles Clements: Swansea, November 25 1961;
Phoenix Opera: Ackworth, Yorkshire, November 23 1963, etc; Arena Opera: 1978; Opera libera: Clandon Park, November 1985
The Lady of Flowers (*Blodeuedd*), dramatic chamber opera in two acts (1981)
[libretto by Alun Cooper based on a story from the Mabinogion (Math vab Mathonwy)]
for three singers, one silent part and piano: approx. 43-45 minutes;
commissioned by Arena Opera with funds provided by the Welsh Arts Council;
Arena Opera: University of Essex Theatre, Colchester, September 17 1982
— additional arias and other material composed, and part added for counter tenor (1991)
4 minutes [additional words by composer and Evelyn Nicholson]

Miscellaneous Works

Music for Shell documentary films (1946)
  (a) *Cine-Magazine* (not recorded)
  (b) *The Single Point Fuel Injector* (string quartet and piano)
  (c) *Air Display* (string quartet)
Incidental music for *Prince Hywel's Last Poem* (1951)
  BBC radio feature by Sir H Idris Bell;
  broadcast, BBC Welsh Service, July 11 1952
Music for two ballets, Pembroke Pageant (1958)
  (a) using *Dadl Dau, Hofedd Hywel, Abergenny* and dramatic links;
  (b) using *Selly Oak Squabble* from *Maid in Birmingham*; fanfares and procession
  21 minutes ($10^1/_2 + 10^1/_2$)
Ian Parrott's Attempt (1962)
  music for string orchestra in the style of Philidor, Monsigny and Grétry;
  40 bars (60 with repeats); to go with *The Music of 'An Adventure'* (see under 'Books')

with Mervyn Burtch, Kenneth Gange and Leonard Pugh:

Gelli Aur, Variations on *Llanymddyfri* (1972)
  November 10, 1972

Arrangements and Editions

Stravinsky: *Ronde des Princesses*
  transcribed for flute, violin, cello and piano (1935); 4 minutes
Overture on Swedish themes :
  arranged for Isis Orchestra, Oxford (1936)
Bach: Two chorale preludes
  transcribed for small orchestra (*The Old Year and the New*) (1936)
Bartók: String Quartet No.4, slow movement
  arranged for organ (1937)
Warlock: *Bethlehem Down*
  accompaniment arranged for small orchestra (1937)
Dibdin: Three songs
  edited (1950), including **Nothing Like Grog** (**Curwen**, 1953)
Schumann: Two pieces from *Manfred*
  arranged for string orchestra (1956)
Schumann: Study for pedal piano No.3
  arranged as *Etude* for oboe, clarinet and piano (1957); **Chappell**, 1964
Bach: Two chorale preludes from *Das Orgel-Büchlein*
  Ich ruf' zu dir, Herr Jesu Christ (BWV639); *Herr Gott, nun Schleuss den Himmel auf* (BWV617)
  arranged for cello and piano (1962); **Novello/Elkin**, 1963;
  dedicated to William Pleeth: broadcast, March 7 1964
Hen Wlad fy Nhadau and *God Save the Queen*
  arranged for Aberystwyth & District Silver Band (and UCW Orchestra) (1971)
Rosemary Brown: Symphony in F minor (from Beethoven)
  orchestration of second movement (1976); approx. 5 minutes; **Basil Ramsey**, 1976;
  NOS, Holland, September 26 1976
  [first movement orchestrated by Alan Hovhaness, October 30 1975]
Rosemary Brown: Two movements (from Mozart), *allegro* and *moderato*
  edited (1977); 13 minutes (10 + 3)

Fauré: *Requiem*
　preface and editing for reprint by **UMP** for Hamelle et cie (1981)
Bach: *Bist du bei mir* (BWV508)
　arranged for cello and piano (1987); 2½ minutes
　— **arranged for euphonium (B flat) and piano** (1993); **Samuel King**, 1994
Schumann: Three Canonic Studies for pedal piano
　arranged for recorder, violin and piano (1998); 13 minutes (4½ + 2 + 6½);
　dedicated to Tom Pitfield;
　John Turner: Bowdon, October 5 1998

Appendix 5

Recordings

A Composer Talks: Modern Harmony (1958) :
  Qualiton, QMP2031 [*LP*]; 27 minutes; sleeve note by Sir Thomas Armstrong
Contemporary Welsh Choral Music (1969) :
  Horizon Recordings, Swansea [*LP*]; for the Guild for the Promotion of Welsh Music;
  Seiriol Singers conducted by John Hywel;
  includes *The Song of the Stones of St Davids*
Music for Harp & Flute (1970) :
  Ars Nova Ars Antiqua, USA [*LP*];
  includes *Ceredigion* for harp played by Phyllis Schlomovitz
Contemporary Welsh Chamber Music (1971) :
  Lyrita, SRCS 52 [*LP*]; University Ensemble of Cardiff;
  includes *String Quartet No.4*
Trumpets Wild (1972) :
  Polydor, 2485 014 [*LP*]; The Cory Band conducted by Major H A Kenney;
  includes *Fantasia, Land of Song*
William Shepherd Plays Trombone (1974) :
  Coronet, Stereo 3001 (USA) [*LP*]; with Lima Symphony Orchestra;
  includes *Trombone Concerto*
The Music of Ian Parrott (1997) :
  TABIP1 [*CD*]; 70 minutes; recorded at Machynlleth Tabernacl;
  John Turner (recorder), Alison Wells (soprano), Keith Swallow (piano)
  includes *Absence, I Heard a Linnet Courting, Westerham, In Phaeacia,*
  Theme and Six Variants, Flamingoes, Arabesque and Dance,
  Two Thoughtful Songs, Happiness, Awel Dyfi,
  The Wrexham Pipers meet the Machynlleth Marchers and *Songs of Renewal,*
  with tributes from Anthony Gilbert, Geoffrey Bush and David Cox
Welsh Classical Favourites (1999) :
  MDT Marco Polo, 8.225048 [*CD*]
  includes *Fanfare-Overture for a Somerset Festival*
Christmas Carols from the Liverpool Phil (1999) :
  L19BP [*CD*]
  includes *The Christ Child*
English Recorder Music (2000) :
  Olympia, OCD667 [*CD*]; Royal Ballet Sinfonia
  includes *Prelude and Waltz for recorder and string orchestra*

Appendix 6

Writings, etc

Books

Pathways to Modern Music [Arthur Unwin, 1947]
A Guide to Musical Thought (1949) [Dobson, Music Students' Library, 1955]
Method in Orchestration [Dobson, 1957]
The Music of 'An Adventure' (1962) [Regency Press, 1966]
The Spiritual Pilgrims (1964)
   Miss Gwendoline Davies, CH, and Miss Margaret Davies, LlD, of Gregynog
   and their Patronage of Music
   with Introduction by Sir Adrian Boult [Christopher Davies, 1969]
Elgar [Dent, Master Musicians Series, 1971]
The Music of Rosemary Brown [Regency Press, 1978]
Hanes yr Urdd er Hyrwyddo Cerddoriaeth Cymru
   The Story of the Guild for the Promotion of Welsh Music, 1955-80
   [Salesbury Press, Llandybie, 1980]
Cyril Scott and His Piano Music [Thames/Wm Elkin, 1992]
The Crying Curlew: Peter Warlock, Family and Influences
   [Gomer, Llandysul, Ceredigion, 1994; Wm Elkin, Nov 2001]

Articles

'An Aspect of Bach', *The Musical Times*, December 1939
'Parry or Puccini?', *The Musical Times*, August 1940
'Musician in the Army', *OCTU Magazine*, Aldershot, May 1941
'Arthur Sullivan, 1842-1900', *Music and Letters*, July 1942
'Metamorphosis', *The Musical Times*, June 1943
'The Style of Bach', *The Musical Times*, September 1945
'Can Good Orchestral Music Pay?', *The Contractors Record*, December 1945
   reprinted in *The Musical Digest*, November 1947
'Encouragement for New Composers', *The Musical Times*, February 1946
'Sir Hugh Allen, an Appreciation', *Making Music*, May 1947
'This Schönbergery', *Keynote*, August 1947

'What is Inspiration?', *Music Parade*, September 1948
'Musical Half-Truths', *Fanfare* (Birmingham School of Music), April 1949
'Bach the Master', *Music Parade*, May 1950
'Imaginary Roots', *Music Teacher*, January 1951
'Psychical Research: Experiences of a Composer',
   The Birmingham Post, August 31 1951
'A Plea for Schumann's Op 11', *Music and Letters*, January 1952
'Words, Music and Meaning', *Music*, Vol.1, No.2, January 1952
'Musicologist or Composer?', *Fanfare*, January 1953
'Celebrity Concert', *Music*, November 1953
'Some Notes on Berwald', *The Musical Times*, May 1954
'Welsh Music from Within or Without', *The Welsh Anvil*, December 1954
'Changed Notes', *The Musical Times*, June 1955
'Variation for a Dog?', *Music Teacher*, January 1956
'The Black Ram', *Dock Leaves*, May 1956
'Escape to Outer Darkness', *The Musical Times*, June 1956
'Writing a New Welsh Opera', *Radio Times* (Welsh edition), February 22 1957
'Was Elgar's Orchestration Impeccable?', *The Chesterian*, *191*, Summer 1957
'The Feeling for Speed', *Music Teacher*, April 1958
'Die Walisische Eisteddfod', *Musica*, July-August 1958
The Coventry Madonna and Bach', *The Musical Times*, August 1959
'The Group Mind', *Light*, Vol.LXXIX No.3441, April 1960
'Globetrotting', *The Western Mail*, January 14 1961
'Measuring Up', *The Western Mail*, March 4 1961
'Compulsory Music', *Music Teacher*, April 1961
   reprinted (cut) in *The Western Mail*, July 29 1961, as 'Piped Torture Around the World'
'Getting Together', *The Western Mail*, January 20 1962
   (on ISM conference in Bristol)
'On the Professional Road', *The Western Mail*, September 8 1962
'Living a Full Life', *The Western Mail*, December 2 1962
'Contrasts? Bach and Wagner', *Music Teacher*, December 1962
'God's Point of View', *St David's Diocesan Gazette*, January 1964, No.140
'Warlock in Wales', *The Musical Times*, October 1964
'The Music of William Mathias',
   The Anglo-Welsh Review, Vol.14, No.34, Winter 1964-65
'Composer with the Common Touch (Gordon Jacob aged 70)',
   The Western Mail, July 14 1965
'Warlock and the Fourth', *Music Review*, May 1966
'The Motets of J S Bach', *Welsh Music*, November 1966
'A Summer Weekend at Gregynog' (extracted from *The Spiritual Pilgrims*)
   The Anglo-Welsh Review, Vol.16, No.37, Spring 1967
'More Compulsory Music', *Music Teacher*, April 1967
'Holst's *Savitri* and Bitonality', *Music Review*, Vol.28, No.4, November 1967
'Fugue without Tears', *Music Teacher*, July 1970
'Elgar's Two-Fold Enigma: a Religious Sequel', *Music and Letters*, January 1973
'Iolanthe', *Music Review*, Vol.34, No.1, February 1973
'Personal View', *The Western Mail* (four articles), 1973
'The Artful Critic: a Rejoinder', *Welsh Music*, Spring 1975
'Another Personal Credo', *Musical Opinion*, October 1975
'Elgar and Bach', *Elgar Society Newsletter*, June 1976

'Questions for Materialists', *Two Worlds* (nine articles), April-December 1977
'Elgar', in *Makers of Modern Culture* [Routledge & Kegan Paul, 1979]
'The Case for the Spiritual View Today',
  The Modern Churchman, Vol.XXII/2 & 3, 1979
'Terminal is not the End', *Two Worlds*, 1981
'Heresies of our Time', *The Modern Churchman*, Vol.XXIV/2, Summer 1981
'Thou shalt not kill', *The Welsh Churchman*, December 1982
  see Foreword to *Life Unlimited* (Allan Barham) under 'Miscellaneous'
'Grove and the Long-Suffering Celtic Composers', *Musical Opinion*, April 1983
'The Enigma V', in *An Elgar Companion*, ed. Christopher Redwood
  [Sequoia, 1983]
'Musician of Distinction, a Tribute to Charles Clements MBE, 1898-1983',
  The Western Mail, April 23 1983
'Influences on my Music', *Musical Opinion*, April 1983
'Thirty-Three Years in Welsh Music', *Welsh Music*, Vol.7, No.3, Spring 1983
'Sir Adrian Boult (1889-1983): a Personal Tribute', *Welsh Music*, Spring 1983
'Some Notes on Elgar in Wales', *Welsh Music*, Vol.7, No.7, Summer 1984
'Why did Beethoven write for the Cello in the treble clef to sound down an octave?',
  Music Review, 1986
'A Musician's Credo', in *Education in Beliefs and Values*
  [Farmington Institute for Christian Studies, 1986]
'Elgar's Harmonic Language', in *Elgar Studies*, ed. R Monk [Scolar, 1990]
'Why Background Music?', *ISM Music Journal*, December 1991
'My Memories of William Mathias', *ISM Music Journal*, September 1992
'The Jolly Shepherd', in *Peter Warlock*, ed. D Cox and J Bishop
  [Thames/Wm Elkin, 1994]
'Elgar and Peter Warlock', *Elgar Society Journal*, May 1994
'Was Warlock Frightened of the Double Bass?',
  Peter Warlock Society Newsletter No.55, Autumn 1994
'The Reputation of Cyril Scott', *Music Review*, November 1993, appeared 1996
  (reprinted from MBS, Sydney, 1992)
'Peter Warlock's *Away to Twiver* and His Honour Lionel Jellinek',
  Peter Warlock Society Newsletter No.59, Autumn 1996
'The Death of Peter Warlock', *Fanfare II*, Birmingham, December 1997
'*The Apostles* - Elgar, "the first English progressive musician" ',
  Elgar Society Journal, early 2003

Lectures & Radio Talks

'The Later Piano Music of Edvard Grieg',
  BBC Home Service (*Music Magazine*), June 15 1947
'Unfinished Fugue?' (Bach in C minor), BBC Third Programme, July 5 1947
'The Mind of the Creative Artist', Trinity College, London, September 29 1948
  (and at Birmingham University, Extra-Mural, March 7 1949)
'Some Aspects of Modern Music', Putney, January 21 1949
'Grieg', BBC General Overseas Service (*Composer of the Week*),
  November 9/10 1952 (recorded October 29)
'Modern Music', Dolgellau, November 18 1952
  (and at Carmarthen, February 12 1954; and Harlech, August 1954)

'Folk Music', Broneirion, Llandinam, April 3 1954
'Opera', Attingham Park, August 1954
'Elgar's *Kingdom* and *Apostles*',
    BBC Home Service (*Music Magazine*), May 26 1957
5-minute talk on travels, BBC Welsh Service (*Mosaics*), March 8 1961
Four talks on NZBC, July-August 1970
'Elgar's Enigma Solved', University of Canterbury, NZ, September 4 1970,
    public lecture (the first of many); also BBC talk, 1972
'The Direction of University Music', BBC (*The Faculty of Music*), 1972
'Sir Henry Walford Davies', Temple Church, London, February 10 1986,
    illustrated lecture for the Hon Soc of Cymmrodorion
    (with Sir George Thalben-Ball, aged 91, unable to play the organ)

Miscellaneous

Revision of *Harmony* (Holmes & Karn) and *Key* to same, June 1951
Programme notes for Beethoven concert, London Philharmonic Orchestra,
    Royal Festival Hall, London, September 17 1958
Review of *The Invention and Composition of Music* (Arthur Hutchings),
    Durham University Review, LII No.1, December 1959
Programme notes for Tchaikovsky concert, London Philharmonic Orchestra,
    Royal Albert Hall, London, January 23 1960
Programme notes for Silk Congress concert, Royal Festival Hall, London, January 1961
Programme notes for Beethoven concert,
    Royal Festival Hall, London, September 29 1961
Review of *NAD* (D Scott Rogo),
    Journal of the Society for Psychical Research, November 1970
Appendix 2, for *Immortals at my Elbow* (Rosemary Brown) [Bachman & Turner, 1974]
Review of *William Mathias* (Malcolm Boyd) (*Composers of Wales No.1*, UWP),
    The Anglo-Welsh Review, No.65, September 1979
Preface to *Stranger than Fiction* (Allan Barham), July 1980
Foreword to *Life Unlimited* (Allan Barham) [Voltuma Press, David Ellis, 1982]
    (see also article: *Thou shalt not kill*, December 1982)
Contribution to *Look Beyond Today* (Rosemary Brown), July 1985
Review of *Writing for the Pedal Harp* (Ruth K Inglefield & Lon A Neill)
    [University of California Press], *Music Review*, March 1987
Programme notes for Swansea Festival concert (GPWM), Bryn Terfel, October 6 1989
Review of Holst's *The Mystic Trumpeter*, *Music Review*, September 1991
Review of *Music for Wales* (David Ian Allsobrook) [University of Wales Press],
    Welsh Journal of Education, November 1992
    (book includes references to *Spiritual Pilgrims*)
Programme note for Elgar's *The Dream of Gerontius*, Aber Choral Society, March 1995
Programme note for City of Birmingham Symphony Orchestra,
    Bartók's *Four Orchestral Pieces*, Symphony Hall, Birmingham, February 18 1997

Contributions to *Die Musik in Geschichte und Gegenwart* on:
    D'Oyly Carte (1953)   J Fawcett (1953)
    Edward German (1954)   Heseltine-Warlock (1955)
    Daniel Jones (1957)   David de Lloyd (1959)
    Sullivan (1961)   Vaughan Thomas (1966)
    Walisische Musik (1967)

Index

Aberystwyth Festival: 60
Aberystwyth Philomusica: 36
Adler, Alfred: 20
Allchin, Basil: 10
Allen, Sir Hugh: 11, 17, 66
Allt, Wilfred Greenhouse: 29
Alwyn, William:
—*Seascapes*: 69
Anderson, Emily (Amy): 26
Andrew, Andrew: 5
Andrews, H K: 66
Angell, Sir Norman: 18
Anglo-Welsh Review, The: 62
Aotearoa Maori Group: 44
ap Huw, Robert: 40
Aprahamian, Felix: 72
ap Rice, Philip: 2
Aquinas, St Thomas: 36
Arányi, Jelly d': 55
Arbeau, Thoinot:
—*Orchésographie*: 32
Armstrong, Sir Thomas: 17
Ashdown, Lord (Sir Paddy Ashdown): 34, *34*
Ashkenazy, Vladimir: 30
Atkins, Sir Ivor: 21, 22
Attingham Park College, Shropshire: 46, 57

Bach, J S: 7, 9, 10, 13, 39, 63-65
—*Bist du bei mir*: 36
—*Mass in B minor*: 9, 12, 64
—*Nun ist das Heil und die Kraft*: 64-65
—*Orgelbüchlein*: 63
—*St Matthew Passion*: 64-65
—*Sheep May Safely Graze*: 19
—*Violin Concerto in A minor*: 8
Bachauer, Gina: 25
Bacon, Francis: 64
Baldwyn, Rodney: 41
Barbanell, Maurice: 47
Barbirolli, Sir John: 18, 40, 54
Barham, Rev. Allan: 41, 47 n.7
Barnes, Mary: 3

Barrett, A G: 3
Bartók, Béla: 10, 15, 20-21, 58
—*Music for Strings, Percussion and Celesta*: 20
—*Piano Concerto No.2*: 15
Bate, Jennifer: 42
Bax, Sir Arnold:
—*Symphony No.3*: 15-16
BBC Scottish Symphony Orchestra: 53
BBC Welsh Symphony Orchestra: 30, 31, 41, 55, 58
Beckwith, John: 49
Beddoes, Thomas Lovell: 38
Beecham, Sir Thomas: 59
Beethoven, Ludwig van: 6, 16, 20, 26, 46
—*Mass in D*: 17
Bell, Sir Idris: 40, 41, 53
Bennett, Elinor: 41
Berg, Alban: 15
Berkeley, Sir Lennox: 22
—*Domini est Terra*: 22
Berkeley, Mary: 1
Berlioz, Hector: 5, 15
Biggs, Teddy: 18
Birmingham Post, The: 45
Blackford, John Richard (grandfather): 5, 7
Blackford, Mary Amelia Louisa (née Tuck) (grandmother): 5
Blake, William: 46
Bliss, Sir Arthur: 11, 52, 55
—*Clarinet Quintet*: 49
—*Music for Strings*: 14
Blow, John:
—*Venus and Adonis*: 17
Bohana, Roy: 36, 55
Boorman, Peter: 41
Bor, Edward: 51
Border, Richard: 22
Boult, Sir Adrian: 29, 40, 41, 55, 56
Bournemouth Symphony Orchestra Shakespeare Prize: 77
Bowen, Dora: 9
Bowen, Kenneth: 46, 52, *54*, 58

Brahms, Johannes: 8, 9, 49
— *Symphony No.3*: 8
Breton, André: 19-20
Brewster, Kingman: 56
Bridges, Mrs Robert: 14
Bridges Scholarship, Margaret: 14, 66
Brinkwells Cottage: 32, 72
British Oxygen Company: 5
Bromley Parish Church: 24
Bromsgrove Festival: 42
Bron Castell, Capel Bangor: 52
Brown, James Murray: 61
Brown, Rosemary: 46, 47 n.10, 57
Brymer, Jack: 72
Buck, Sir Percy: 10-12
Burtch, Mervyn: 58
Bush, Geoffrey: 61
Butler, Samuel: 12

Cadarn, Thomas: 2
Cagney, James: 16
Cairo Radio: 39
Carew Castle: 2
Carl Rosa Opera Company: 15, 59
Cefn Bryntalch: 67
Chaliapin, Fyodor: 11
Challinor, Jack & Peggy: 52
Charles, HRH Prince: 57, 59-60
Cheltenham Festival: 41
Chesterian, The: 45
Chopin, Frederic: 6, 7, 11, 46, 74, 75
Chroustchoff, Boris de: 74
Chroustchoff, Igor & Natasha: 74
Churchill, Sir Winston: 26
Clapham, John: 51
Clarke, Alice, Jane & Margaret: 4
Clarke, Nindi: 19
Cleaver, Emrys: 41, 55
Clements, Charles: 51, 52, 54, 55, 57-58
Cohen Musicology Award, Harriet: 56, 72
Colles, H C: 10
Coates, Albert: 12, 13
Cockshott, Gerald: 72
Cocteau, Jean: 19
Coghill, Neville: 17
Composers Guild of Great Britain: 70
Cook, E T: 10
Cook, John: 49
Cooper Joseph: 13
Copley, Ian: 66, 72
Coventry Cathedral: 63ff
Cox, David: 18, 88
— *Mr Playford's Musical Banquet*: 69
Cox, Edwin (father-in-law): 23-24
Cox, Olga (née Ilinsky) (mother-in-law): 23-24

Crum, Michael: 17

Dale, Benjamin: 7
Davies, Carol: 58
Davies, George: 37
Davies CH, Gwendoline: 52, 57, 59
Davies, Sir H Walford: 13, 52, 56, 58
Davies, Hubert: 60
Davies, John S: 36
Davies, Dr Lyn: 37, 74
Davies LLD, Margaret: 52, 57, 59
Davies, Canon Walter Emlyn: 57
Davies of Llandinam, The Lady: 55
Davies of Llandinam, The Third Lord: 59
Davison, John: 20
Delacroix, Ferdinand: 46
Delius, Frederick: 10, 13, 59
Denison, John: 11
Diab, Salma: 25
Dock Leaves: 62
Donne, John: 38
Dorian Trio: 60
Dreikurs, Rudolf: 20
Dunhill, Thomas:
— *Tantivy Towers*: 8
Dulova, Vera: 41
Dunstable, John: 63
Dussek, Winifred: 18, 67
Dykes Bower, John: 11
Dyson, Sir George: 12
— *Nebuchadnezzar*: 16-17

Eaton, Eunice: 39
Edwards, Canon Emrys: 60
Edwards, John: 30, 31, 40, 54, 55
Edwards, Owain: 57
Elgar, Sir Edward: 13, 15, 18, 32, 33, 44, 47 n.4, 52, 56
— *Dream of Gerontius, The*: 16, 52
— *Enigma Variations*: 21 (*Troyte*), 35, 56
— *In Smyrna*: 69
Elgar Society, The: 22 n.5, 37, 56, 73
Elizabeth II, HM Queen: 54
Ellis, Osian: 41
Elwyn-Edwards, Dilys: 61
Evans, Gaynor (Mrs Hall): 53
Evans, Sir Geraint: 32
Evans, Ifor L: 51, 52, 57
Evans, Ivor & Elsie: 51
Evans, J Glynne: 62

Faulkner, Keith: 15
Ferland, Captain Armand: 49
Filer, Jayne: 53
Fiocco, Joseph-Hector: 8
Fishguard Festival: 36

Flecker, James Elroy: 45
Flew, Anthony: 45
Foster, Arnold: 72
Franck, César: 8, 52
Franklin, John: 3
Freud, Sigmund: 19-20

Gade, Niels: 9
Gange, Kenneth: 58
Garcia, Albert: 10
Garcia, Manuel: 10
Gaskell, Winifred: 11
George V, HM King: 11
George, Stefan: 35
Gibbs, C Armstrong: 20-21, 22 n.6
Gilbert, Norman: 72
Gilbert, W S: 8, 20
—*The Gondoliers*: 31
Glazunov, Alexander: 15, 67
—*Symphony No.6*: 15, 67
Glyn, Gareth: 60
Godfrey, Sir Dan: 11
Gray, Cecil: 17, 18, 67
Gregynog Chair of Music, Aberystwyth: 29, 51, 70
Gregynog Festival: 52
Grétry, André-Ernest-Modeste: 46
Griffith, Troyte: 21
Griffiths, Ann: 41
Griffiths, Vernon: 44, 48, 49, 55, 71
Griller String Quartet: 15
Groves, Sir Charles: 10, 11, 22 n.4
Guild for the Promotion of Welsh Music: 30-37, 40, 47 n.2, 54, 55, 56, 62 n.1

Hallé Orchestra: 40, 41, 54
Handel, George Frederic: 11
Harries, David: 37 n.1, 56, 58, 60
—*Violin Concerto*: 31, 60
Harrison, John: 60
Harrow, 14 Kenton Road: 5
—South House, Flambard Road: 6
Harrow School: 7ff, *8*, 79
Havard, Royston: 41
Healey, E G: 52
Hembrey, Basil: 20
Henry VIII: 1
Henshall, Dalwyn: 60
Hillier, Lucy: 5
Hindemith, Paul: 48
HMS Hood: 9, 16
Hoddinott, Alun: 32, 40, 49, 54, 60, 61, 62
Holmes, Marcus: 9
Holst, Gustav: 8, 11, 13, 16, 39
—*Humbert Wolfe Songs*: 69
Honegger, Arthur: 21

Hook, William: 10, 15, 18
Hopkins, Delyth: 59
Hopkins, Gerard Manley: 46
Howes, Frank: 72
Huggill, Henry: 17
Hughes, Arwel: 30, 40, 55, 58, 61
Hulme, David Russell: 36
Hutchings, Arthur: 66
Huxley, Aldous: 17, 20

Iago, John: 8, 9
Ibert, Jacques:
—*L'Aiglon*: 18
Ilinsky, Olga: see Cox
Incorporated Society of Musicians: 31, 37, 71, 72
International Society for Music Education: 55
Isis Orchestra, Oxford: 15, 67

Jacob, Gordon: 61
Jacobson, Maurice: 17
Jacoby, Robert: 58
James, Leonard (Bill): 58
Jellinek, His Honour Lionel: 74
Jenkins, Rae: 71, 77
Jeremy, Raymond: 52
John, Geraint: 58
Jones, Arthur Hefin: 52
Jones, Sir Bryner: 52
Jones, Daniel: 32, 54, 60, 62
Jones, Delme Bryn: 60
Jones, Elwyn: 58
Jones, Glanville: 32
Jones, Glynne: 32
Jones, Gwladys Morgan: 55
Jones, J Alwyn: 58
Jones, Lewis: 16
Jones CH, Dr Thomas: 52
Jourdain, Eleanor: 45-46, 67
Juilliard School of Music, New York: 48

Kerner, Justinus: 38
Keys, Ivor: 11, 58
King, MacDougall: 20
Kingsley, Colin: 61
Kingswood, Peter: 58
Kipnis, Alexander: 15
Kirby String Quartet: 18, 67
Kitson, Charles H: 10, 12
Kitson, Elizabeth: 18, 67
Kodály, Zoltán:
—*Háry János*: 15
Kutcher String Quartet: 15

Lambert, Captain & Mrs Richard and Ruth:

Lambert, Constant: 15, 67
—*Rio Grande, The*: 54
Le Fleming, Christopher: 72
Lemare, Iris: 11
Lermontov, Mikhail: 38
Lewis, Anthony: 29
Lewis, Enid: 60
Lewis, Geraint: 36
Lewis, Logan: 51
Ley, Henry: 10, 12
Listener, The: 45
Liszt, Franz: 6, 15
Llanbadarn Church: 32, 33, 53, 57, 60
Llandeilo School Orchestra: 58
Llewellyn, Redvers: 54, 55, 59
Llewelyn, David: 58
Lloyd, David de: 52, 57, 62
Locke, Matthew:
—*Macbeth*: 15
Lokey, Hamilton: 57
London Opera Centre: 27
London Philharmonic Orchestra: 29, 40, 41
London Symphony Orchestra: 40, 53
Long, Kathleen: 15
Luther, Martin: 35

Mabinogion: 42
MacDowall, Captain William: 22 n.1
Machynlleth Festival: 36
MacLean, Quentin: 9, 13
Maeterlinck, Maurice: 36
Malcolmson, Kenneth: 14
Malvern College: 18ff
Mangeot, André: 66
Manning, Edward: 18, 67
Markova Ballet: 17
Masefield, John: 16, 33
Mathias, William: 54, 55, 58, 61, 62
Mendelssohn, Felix: 16
—*Elijah*: 13, 20
Menges, Isolde: 8
Menuhin, Lord (Yehudi Menuhin): 31, 53
Middleton, H S: 61
Mid-Wales Youth Orchestra: 71
Miller, Robin: 10, 13, 18, 67
Mills, Patrick: 37, 67
Moberly, Miss C A E: 67
Monsigny, Pierre Alexandre: 46
Monteverdi, Claudio:
—*Vespro della Beata Virgine (1610)*: 53
Montgomery County Music Festival: 54
Montgomery of Alamein, First Viscount: 25. 26
Moore, Jerold Northrop: 73

Morris, Wyn: 41
Morton, Prof V C: 57
Morus, Huw: 41
Moy, Edgar: 29
Mozart, W A: 12, 26
—*Don Giovanni*: 59
—*Nozze di Figaro, Le*: 23
Mulgan, Denis: 13-15, 17, 18, 20, 22, 23, 67
Musica: 62
Musical Opinion: 47 n.5
Musical Times, The: 21, 47 n.3, 47 n.6, 62
Music and Letters: 40
Music Teacher: 47 n.1, 47 n.6
Musik in Geschichte und Gegenwart: 53
Mussorgsky, Modest: 53

Nabarro, F: 17
Narberth Castle: 1
National Band of New Zealand: 44
National Brass Band Championships: 79
National Eisteddfod: 40, 53, 58
National Library of Wales: 54
Neel, Boyd: 49
Neighbour, Alice: 3, 4
Neill, Andrew: 36
Netherlands Radio Philharmonic Orchestra: 46
Neuburg, Victor: 32
New College, Oxford: 11ff, 66
Newton, Lily: 57
New York Town Hall: 39
New Zealand Opera Company: 27
Nicholson, Ralph: 11
Nikisch, Arthur: 12
North Wales Festival, St Asaph: 36, 41

Ogdon, John: 30
Old Tithe Barn, West Lancing: 23-24
Opera da Camera: 55
Orley Farm Preparatory School: 6, 35, 66
Owen, Gwawr: 60
Oxford Harmonic Society: 66
Oxford University Gazette: 24

Paderewski, Ignacy: 11
Palestrina, Giovanni Pierluigi da: 66
Palmer, Charles: 14
Parrett Festival: 34
Parrott, Charles Montague: 5
Parrott, Cynthia (sister): 6
Parrott, Elizabeth (née Cox) (first wife): 23-24, 29, 30, 32, 33, 42, 46, 53, 56, 57, 61
Parrott, Horace Bailey (father): 4-6, 4, 8, 14, 18

Parrott, Hugh MacDowall: 5, 18
Parrott, Ian:
—*Arabesque and Dance* [1972]: 69
—*Arfon* [1978]: 41, *86*
—*Aspects* [1975]: 68
—*Awel Dyfi* [1995]: 69
—*Black Ram, The* [1951-53]: 40, 53, 54, 55, 56, 62
—*Ceredigion* [1957]: 41
—*Dair, Y (The Three Ladies)* [1958]: 41
—*Dream, A* [1941]: 24, 45
—*El Alamein* [1944]: 53
—*Fanfare-Overture* [1993]: 34, *80-81*
—*Fantasy and Allegro* [1946]: 46, 60
—*Flamingoes* [1972]: 61, 68
—*Four Songs of Absence* [1942-44]: 38
—*I Heard a Linnet Courting* [1943]: 68
—*In Phaeacia* [1945]: 45
—*Luxor* [1947]: 26, 29, 39, 40, 53
—*Oboe Sonata* [1935-36]: 17
—*Once Upon a Time* [1956-59]: 50, *54*
—*Pant Glas* [1967]: 46
—*Percyisms* [2000]: 91
—*Portraits* [1999]: *107*
—*Psalm 91* [1946]: 24
—*Reaching for the Light* [1971]: 46, 57
—*Scherzo I* [1933]: 15
—*Seithenin Overture* [1959]: 41
—*Sergeant-Major's Daughter, The* [1942-43]: 26, 39
—*Sinfonietta (Symphony No.4)* [1978]: 46
—*Songs of Renewal* [1995]: 33, 68
—*Symphony No.1* [1946]: 45
—*Symphony No.2* [1960]: 42, 50
—*Symphony No.3* [1966]: 44, 58
—*Symphony No.5* [1979]: 46
—*Theme and Six Variants* [1945]: 39
—*Three Thoughtful Songs* [1977]: 46, 68
—*Wind Quintet No.2* [1970]: 42-44, *43*
—*Variations on 'The Last Rose of Summer'* [1933]: 12
—*Welsh Folk Song Mass* [1972]: 58
—*Westerham* [1940]: 24, 69
Parrott, James: 3
Parrott, Jeanne (née Harrison, formerly Peckham) (second wife): 33, 37, *37*, *92*
Parrott, Joseph Erichson (grandfather): 1, 4
Parrott, Joseph Reginald: 5
Parrott, Michael (son): 29, *34*, 71
Parrott, Muriel Annie (née Blackford) (mother): 5, 6, *6*, 11, 18, 29
Parrott, William Alfred Erichson: 3, 5
Parry, Joseph: 59
Parry-Williams, Sir Thomas: 40, 53, 57
Pasfield, Bill: 32

Payne, Anthony: 72
Payzant, Geoffrey: 49
Pendyrus Male Voice Choir: 32
Perrot, Sir Andrew: 1
Perrot, George (Yorkshire): 3
Perrott, Augustus Alfred (great-grandfather): 3-4
Perrott, Benjamin Goddard: 3
Perrott, Clement: 3
Perrott, George (Haroldston): 3
Perrott, Sir John: 1-3
Perrott, Sir Richard: 3
Perrott, Robert: 1, 3
Perrott, Simon: 3
Perrott, Sir Thomas: 1
Perrott, William: 3
Perrott, William de: 1
Pershore Abbey: 41
Petts, John: 32
Pfitzner, Hans: 14
Philidor, François André: 46
Phillips, J B: 35
Pleeth, William: 41
Polin, Claire: 48
Pope, Michael: *73*
Popov, Stefan: 87
Porcelijn, David: 46
Price, Cecil: 50, *54*
Price, Richard Maldwyn: 58, 60
Pring, Phillip Henry & Dorothy May (née Parrott): 5, 18
Prospo, R de: 56
Psychic News: 47
Puccini, Giacomo: 15
—*Gianni Schicchi*: 21
—*Turandot*: 18
Pugh, Leonard: 58
Pullein, William: 7
Purachatra, Prince Prem: 15, 16

Quinnell, Ivan: 30

Ramsey, Basil: 46
Rands, Bernard: 40
Rasmussen, Doreen: 25
Ravel, Maurice: 12
Redlich, Hans: 40, 53, 61
Rees, Goronwy: 57
Richards, Bishop John: 56, 57
Richardson, J: 17
Ritchie, John: 49, 55
Roberts, Trevor: 61
Robertson, James: 27
Robinson, Bernard: 24
Robinson, Christopher: *73*
Ronald, Sir Landon: 11

Rooney, Mickey: 16
Rossini, Gioachino;
—*William Tell Overture*: 25
Roth String Quartet: 15
Rothwell, Evelyn (Lady Barbirolli):
  11, 22 n.5
Rowley, Alec: 29
Royal Canadian College of Organists: 49
Royal College of Music: 8ff, 59, 66
Royal College of Organists: 13
Royal Philharmonic Society Prize: 29, 40
Rubbra, Edmund: 52, 61
Runge, John (Bobbie): 28
Russell, Third Earl (Bertrand Russell): 18
Rutgers University, Camden, USA: 48
Rutland, Harold: 28 n

St Hugh's Choral Society, Oxford: 67
St John's College, Cambridge: 41
St Marks, Venice: 53
St Nicolas College of Church Music,
  Chislehurst: 13, 16
Sayers, Dorothy: 36
Schabas, Ezra: 49
Scherchen, Hermann: 20
Schlomovitz, Phyllis: 41
Schönberg, Arnold: 10, 20
Schubert, Franz: 15
Schuman, William: 48
Scott, Cyril: 33-35
—*Aubade for recorder and piano*: 68
Scott, Sir Walter: 6
Searle, Humphrey: 14, 15, 18, 21, 47, 67
Seithenin, Prince of Dyfed: 78 n
Seymour, Deryck: 10, 11, 16
Shakespeare, William: 64
Shaw, A T: 56
Shaw, George Bernard: 17
Sidebottom, Andrew: 42, 60
Smeterlin, Jan: 18
Smith A E: 67
Smith, A H: 14
Smith, Keith: 34
Smith, Robert: 61
Society for Psychical Research: 45, 70
Sorabji, Kaikhosru Shapurji: 21
Southampton Youth Orchestra: 34
Spicer, Harold: 17
Staatsoper, Dresden: 14
Stainer, Sir John: 11
Stanford, Sir Charles Villiers: 11
Strachan, Norman: 8, 10, 14, 18, 28
Strauss, Richard: 12, 14
—*Ariadne auf Naxos*: 18
Studeny String Quartet: 14
Suddaby, Elsie: 55

Sullivan, Sir Arthur: 8
Sutherland, Halliday: 20
Swallow, Keith: 68-69

Taylor, Leslie: 9
Taylor, Pauline: 60
Tchaikovsky, Peter: 44
—*Symphony No.6*: 8
Tchaikovsky Competition, Moscow: 30
Tenby Arts Festival: 36
Terry, Sir Richard Runciman: 18
Te Wiata, Inia: 44
Thalben-Ball, Sir George: 9
Thatcher, Sir Reginald: 7, 9, 66
Thewlis, George: 67
Thomas, A B: 52, 58
Thomas, A F Leighton: 41, 47 n.3
Thomas, D Vaughan: 61
Thomas, Dylan: 19, 32
Thomas, Eirioes: *54*
Thomas, Mansel: 30, 55, 59, 60, 61
Three Choirs Festival: 16, 22
Till, Maurice: 50
Times, The: 56
Tipoo Sahib: 22 n.1
Tippett, Sir Michael: 56
Todd, Daphne: 74, *74*
Toovey, Michael: 50
Tovey, Sir Donald: 16
Traherne, Sir Cenydd: 55
Trevelyan, Sir George: 46, 57
Trinity College of Music, London:
  27, 28 n, 29, 42, 44, 48, 55
Turner, Dame Eva: 18
Turner, John: 37, 68-69, *92*
Turner, Margaret: *92*
Two Worlds: 47

Union Cold Storage Company: 23
Union of Graduates in Music: 70, 71
University College of Wales, Aberystwyth:
  29ff, 51ff
University of Birmingham: 29, 45
University of Bristol: 56
University of Canterbury, New Zealand:
  44, 48-49, 55
University of Leicester: 56
University of Manchester: 56

Vaughan, Bishop B N Y: 58
Vaughan, Master Richard: 1-2
Vaughan Williams, Ralph: 52
Velasquez, Diego: 12
Verdi, Giuseppe: 15
—*Otello*: 59
Virgil: 13

Virtuoso Ensemble, The: 41
Virtuoso String Quartet: 52

Wade, Frederick: 18, 67
Wagner Richard: 14, 16
—*Die Walküre*: 10
—*Siegfried*: 12
Walker, L: 17
Walker, Ron: *54*
Walton, Sir William: 15
Warlock, Peter (Philip Heseltine):
  15, 17, 18, 32, 33, 66-67, 70, 73
—*Bethlehem Down*: 67
—*Corpus Christi*: 67
—*Curlew, The*: 18, 67
—*Fox, The*: 68
—*Ha'nacker Mill*: 68
—*Lady's Birthday, The*: 18, 67
—*Lillygay*: 67
—*Old Song, An*: 67
—*Pretty Ring Time*: 68
—*Robin Good-Fellow*: 68
—*Three Dirges of Webster*: 18, 67
—*What cheer? Good cheer!*: 66
Warlock Society, The Peter: 37, 72
Watson, Sydney: 15, 66-67
Watt, Howard: 60
Watts, Julie: 36
Weir, Gillian: 42
Wells, Alison: 68-69, *92*

Wells, H G: 16
Welsh Anvil, The: 62
Welsh National Opera: 59

Western Mail, The: 59, 62 n.2
Westminster Abbey: 42, 60
Westrup, Sir Jack: 56
Whitehead, James: 11
Widdop, Walter: 12
Willan, Healey: 49
Williams, Cyril: 59
Williams, Elma: 46, 57
Williams, Grace: 32, 59, 60, 61
Wilson, Dorothy: 52
Wilson, Jane: 46
Winfield, Roger: 41
Wood Frederic: 39
Wood, Sir Henry: 15
Worshipful Company of Musicians: 60
Wray, John: 10, 13, 14
Wynne, David: 60, 61
—*Piano Sonata No.1*: 30

Yale, Elihu: 56
Yale University Concert Band: 78
Yeats, William Butler: 67
Young, Percy: *73*, 91

Zweig, Stefan: 33-34

British Music Society Personnel 2003

President
John McCabe CBE

Vice-Presidents
Richard Arnell
Sir Malcolm Arnold CBE
Dame Janet Baker DBE CH
Richard Baker OBE
Jennifer Bate
Michael Berkeley
Lady Bliss
Sir Colin Davis CH CBE
Giles Easterbrook
Lewis Foreman
Vernon Handley
Tasmin Little
David Lloyd-Jones
Peter Middleton, *Founder Chairman*
Sir Simon Rattle CBE
Malcolm Smith
Basil Tschaikov

Berkeley Medallists
John Dodd
Gerald Leach
Brian Blyth Daubney
Paul Daubney

Executive Committee
Raphael Terroni, *Chairman*
John Talbot, *Vice-Chairman and Recordings Manager*
David Burkett, *Secretary*
Stephen Trowell, *Hon. Treasurer*
Robert Barnett, *Editor 'BMS News'*
Roger Carpenter, *Editor 'British Music'*
Christopher Johns
Tim Mahon
Alastair Mitchell
Malcolm Smith

International Representatives
Jürgen Schaarwächter (*Germany*)
William Marsh (*USA*)